Brats in Keeping Canaries

A guide for the pet canary owner

About this book:

This book is written especially to focus on the needs of the pet canary owner or breeder, especially those new to keeping canaries. It offers help with everything from learning how to choose, house, feed, tame, and care for a single pet, to keeping, breeding, pairing and feeding multiple pairs of canaries, including how to help them reliably raise young.

You will also find a bonus so far found nowhere else in print; an educational series of photos of a pair of canaries raising their babies, from laying the eggs to fledging.

While we are continually learning more about avian ways, there is still much mystery associated with the 'common' canary's living and breeding habits and needs. It is our goal to help clarify some of the basics to successful canary keeping, including the reasons behind certain traditions, so that the new pet owner or breeder can more easily learn how to reap the rewards of owning a happy canary, whether keeping a single pet or a roomful of breeding canaries.

About the Author:

Robirda has been working and living with animals and birds— and writing stories about them— all of her life.

Her feeling of kinship with the natural world extends to plants & wild birds, as well as animals; Robirda loves Nature in all its moods and variation, and is an avid organic gardener and birder, wherever she lives. (Currently, in Westbank, in British Columbia's Okanagan Valley.)

Brats in Feathers; *Keeping Canaries*

Dedicated to all those who spend their lives trying to leave this world a better place than they found it.

Third edition print publication June 2010
by Robirda Online, 9-2065 Boucherie Rd, BC, Canada, V4T-2A7

Based on the website at

www.robirda.com

Copyright © 1995–2010

ISBN: 1453638792

EAN-13: 9781453638798

By Robirda McDonald, with a chapter each by Sharon Klueber & Jim Clever, used with their permission. All rights reserved by the authors.

No part of the text of this book may be edited, reproduced, translated or arranged without written permission of the Author with the exception of short excerpts for the purpose of a book review.

All photographs by R. C. McDonald, unless otherwise noted.
All photos were used with permission of the photographer, are copyrighted by their photographer, and may not be reproduced or copied in any way without permission of the photographer.

Contents

Chapter 1: Consider The Canary   page 05
Chapter 2: Housing Your Canary   page 11
Chapter 3: Finding the Right Canary   page 22
Chapter 4: Basic Canary Care   page 27
Chapter 5: Encouraging Song   page 34
Chapter 6: Taming Your Canary   page 49
Chapter 7: Health & the Avian Vet   page 63
Chapter 8: To Breed or Not To Breed?   page 68
Chapter 9: So, You Want to Breed, Eh?   page 75
Chapter 10: Preparing For Breeding   page 82
Chapter 11: Seasons & The Canary   page 87
Chapter 12: The Breeding Cage   page 93
Chapter 13: Nests & Nest Liners   page 97
Chapter 14: The Incredible Egg   page 101
Chapter 15: Laying Eggs, Raising Chicks   page 108
Chapter 16: Record-Keeping   page 120
Chapter 17: Handling Canaries   page 125
Chapter 18: Handling & Candling Eggs   page 130
Chapter 19: Soak Seed & Nestling Food   page 135
Chapter 20: Pertinent Points on Breeding   page 142
Chapter 21: Weaning Youngsters   page 157
Chapter 22: Basic Canary Colours & Genetics   page 163
Recommended Reading   page 178

Brats in Feathers; *Keeping Canaries*

A group of young canaries playing in one of the author's flights.

Chapter 1
Consider The Canary

The word 'canary' has come into wide use in recent years as a term for describing a person or an animal species who has displayed extreme sensitivity to one or more of the commonly-encountered toxins found everywhere in our modern lives. Often the potential these toxins have for harm is not properly understood until the adverse reactions of the 'canaries' in question impels the undertaking of in-depth studies.

It always astounds me how casually so many people sling the word 'canary' around, while understanding so little about the bird from whom the term sprang. I believe it would benefit all of us greatly, if, in our daily rush to learn and earn, we remember occasionally to consider the canary.

The world of the canary is a tremendous one, and not much at all like the traditional view of the little yellow bird who "just sits in a cage and sings".

They come in every colour of the rainbow, except sky-blues, purples, and black, and can be seen in an almost bewildering array and combination of colours, kinds, sounds, and shapes, all that you can imagine— and probably as many more that you can't.

Many are capable of charming humans with more than just their song— they have been known to develop and express winsome, brassy, confident, confiding and curious personalities. In fact, many canary owners are people who started out with other pets or birds, but upon having acquired their first canary, by whatever happenstance of circumstance or fate, found themselves utterly enthralled by this mysterious and often confusing little ball of feathers.

The wild ancestor of most of our current-day canaries came from the Canary Islands. The various colours that include red or orange in their colouring, sometimes known (incorrectly) as 'red factor' canaries, also count the South American Black-capped Red Siskin in their ancestry, but even *their* genetic code acquires most of its characteristics from the little gray-green birds native solely to one group of Atlantic islands.

Contrary to what many people believe, the birds were actually named after the islands, not the other way around.

Roman naturalist Plinius wrote how Juba, the King of Mauritania, vassal to Rome in the first century BC, sent an expedition to explore the mythical 'Fortunate Islands', said to be located in the 'Dark Ocean' (the Atlantic) beyond 'the Columns of Hercules' (the Strait of Gibraltar).

The islands were indeed there, and the expedition reported finding, exploring, and naming all the islands in the group. Plinius wrote that one of the islands, on which was found a fierce breed of wild dogs (canis in Latin), was named 'Canaria', or, 'Island of Dogs'.

Plinius, however, may have been wrong; the historians of the island today known as 'Gran Canaria' hold that the island's original inhabitants were a tribe who called themselves the 'Canarii'. In the fifteenth century, the island of the Canarii became famous for the brave defense deployed by its natives against repeated attempts at invasion by the conquistadors. They say that it was the conquistadors who began to call the entire island group 'the Islands of the Canaria', from which term eventually came the name under which we know them today, the 'Canary Islands'.

The original canary, while sweet-voiced, was small, and a rather dull gray-green in colour, with black striations. It attracted the notice of some of the fifteenth century Spanish sailors with its confiding ways and freely offered songs. They were quick to take the chance to capture and bring home a few of these charming little songsters.

History— or legend— tells us the intent was to present these little charmers to their ladies fair. From those small beginnings, the species eventually spread worldwide, and spawned literally hundreds of colours, shapes, sounds and kinds of canaries.

A pair of wild canaries; the male is on the right. *(photo by Hans Classen)*

Renowned at first for their song, they were extremely rare and in high demand until the secret of breeding them was worked out. It wasn't long after that before canaries began to make their way into our hearts, our histories, and our cultures.

Once techniques necessary to encourage reproduction

were available, a whole new world of experimentation opened to those involved in breeding canaries. Suddenly it was possible to experiment with how a bird's genetic traits passed from generation to generation, and to observe the results. Song, colour, body shape and size could all be altered to fit the inner vision of the breeder.

Similar techniques had been practiced all along, of course, with regard to other domestic animals and livestock, but when working with species that take years to mature, such experimentation can take several lifetimes to achieve a goal. Canaries, with their one-year-to-maturity breeding cycle, provided exceptionally fast results by comparison.

Contests began to be held, where the birds were judged on singing ability and presentation, or on colour, size, shape, and stance; the variations were almost endless. To own a canary was the height of fashion, and the desire of all.

* * * * * * * * *

Fashion is a fickle mistress; she will take you up in a sudden, breathless rush, then drop you without notice. The Canary's interaction with Lady Fashion lasted several hundred years, but has been under slow decline for the last century.

War decimated entire branches of the species, as their owners marched away to serve their country. The birds were left in the hands of people who had little time to do anything but try to survive. Even if they'd had the time, most had little to no idea of how to provide even basic care, much less apply the skills and techniques required to satisfy the demanding needs of the breeding canary.

When the explorations of the 'newly discovered' lands in the South Pacific brought more small enchanting birds to win the hearts of the public, the decline of the canary as 'the' pet bird to keep inevitable.

Many of these birds (the budgie is a good example) were not only beautiful, small, affectionate and easily tamed, but they also were far easier to maintain and breed, requiring far less demanding care and upkeep. Soon they were available at far cheaper prices than canaries could ever be sold for. Slowly, unnoticed by the majority of the world's population, the canary quietly began to once again become a rarity.

I couldn't tell you how many people I've talked to who "couldn't find a canary anywhere", although they hunted high and low, leaving no stones unturned. After days or weeks of searching, one or maybe two rather bedraggled-looking specimens are turned up. Too many have spent a goodly sum on such a bird, only to have it languish in its cage, never sing, and soon die.

All too often the cages & conditions these birds live in are a result of a lack of understanding of the needs and inclinations of the 'common' canary. Little enough is available in written form about them, these days, and often any interest in canaries is regarded by others as nothing more than a casual hobby.

A variegated Yorkshire Canary, this breed is often called "The Guardsmen of the Fancy" due to their upright posture. *(photo by Hans Classen)*

Canaries nowadays are popularly regarded as sad if somewhat exotic creatures, bred to life in a tiny cage. Most also consider them overly expensive and even boring, good for nothing more than to sit in their cage and sing, or perhaps to serve the purpose of keeping old Aunt Sarah or Uncle Bob happy in his or her dotage.

Yet nothing could be further from the truth.

Understanding more about the 'common' canary could hold an important key to the future of our entire planet. This often-unremarked little bird was used in the past by miners working in coal mines for the same reason it may yet prove to be invaluable in the future— its needs and requirements are similar to those of humankind, but it has far more sensitivity to toxins and chemicals than us— so, any place a canary thrives, is a good place for a human to live too.

If the canaries begin to die, there may still be enough time to escape with your lives. This was the lesson taught to many a miner by the canaries of their time. What they and other similarly sensitive species may yet teach us, as we learn to live— or die— with the rapidly shifting and ever-increasing levels of toxins and chemicals in our planet's atmosphere, has yet to be discovered.

Two of the author's young canaries posing for their photo session.
(photo by Michael de Frietas)

In the meantime, perhaps it is time for us to try to learn more about our canaries, lest in the end we find we have lost, not only them, but the entire spectrum of life they represent— including ourselves, and the rest of our planet.

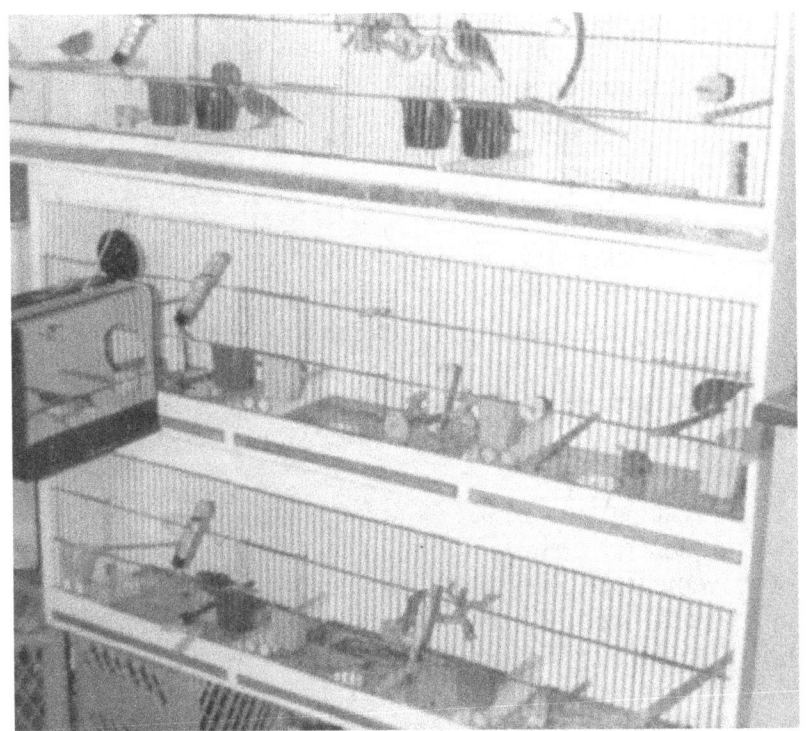

Get youngsters acquainted with the show cage by letting them run freely in and out. Adding treats offers incentive to visit, and acts as a reward too.

Chapter 2
Housing Your Canary

So you've decided you want a canary. But before you go looking for your canary, you will need to get a cage and various assorted provisions and accessories to go with it.

At the very minimum you will need;
- A reasonably sized cage;
- Two drinkers, and four seed cups;
- A small assortment of perches;
- A bird bath to hang on the cage door;
- Paper to line the cage floor;
- A cuttlebone and/or mineral block;
- A balanced avian vitamin supplement;

➤ A clean, fresh seed mix.

Let's go over these items one at a time, in detail.

The Cage:

Far too many new canary owners have ended up with a tall, narrow round cage, totally unsuitable for a canary, often on the recommendation of somebody who had no idea what they were talking of.

A large round cage is preferable to a small square cage, when it comes right down to it— but the fact is that round cages make it very awkward to set up the perches and food dishes so that the canary will be able to use them comfortably.

A canary moves back and forth— this is the most natural way for them to move. In order to facilitate this kind of movement, perches should be paired in parallel on opposite sides of the cage. A round cage makes it difficult if not impossible to set up the perches to allow the bird to move in this manner.

As if that were not enough, round cages are more difficult to clean than rectangular ones, and get dirtier faster. Few people realize this, though, and round cages do look nice to the human eye, as well as being easier to make than the rectangular cages, so both retailers and manufacturers tend to prefer to sell round cages whenever possible.

The fact that these cages are not appropriate for housing birds such as canaries rarely if ever seems to be taken into consideration. This is why it is so important for pet owners to know the difference, and demand that proper cages, made with the bird's needs in mind, be made available at a reasonable price.

Since canaries do not prefer to fly vertically up and down, a rectangular cage should be as wide as possible. I consider 40 inches optimal, but very few pet cages will be found made in this width. However, there are a variety of commercially produced cages that run from 24 to 36 inches long. Many are equally as tall as they are wide, or more— this is not quite as important as width but is nice to have, as it allows your pet more exercise room.

Be careful if you find yourself considering buying galvanized cages or cage-wire; if you buy hot-dipped galvanized metal, you could inadvertently give your birds zinc poisoning. Electroplated galvanized cages cost more, but are far safer than the cheaper hot-dipped galvanized cages.

Seed cups and drinkers:

Try not to get the cages with the closed outside feeders— or if you do, replace them. Removing them can leave gaps, but it is quite simple to wire a small piece of hardware cloth with half inch mesh over the hole. These cups are just not worth the convenience they supposedly offer.

A few of the wide variety of serving cups available to use for your canary, from finger cups to aviary seed cups, including the useful cheap plain paper plate. As long as they are made of safe material and have a safe finish, a variety of dishes can be used for a canary.

Sure, it's nice to be able to check the seed without having to open the cage door— but canaries don't like eating from them, and most are difficult to clean, and fiddly to set up and replace. Even worse, the covered cup greatly increases the chance he could inhale seed dust or a piece of chaff while eating. Such simple beginnings can result in fungal infections or worse, producing some of the most devastating diseases around.

Prevention is simple— buy clean seed, use open cups, and blow the chaff and dust off the seed on a regular basis, daily or oftener. Be sure you don't place the cups under a perch, too!

Refreshing the seed every morning is made simpler if you have double the amount of cups you need; rather than cleaning the cup and replacing it with fresh seed, simply place the new cup with the day's seed into the cage, and remove the old cup to clean at your leisure. Try to use a cup which has no sharp-angled corners— these can trap dirt and dust, and make it more difficult to clean it properly.

The same idea works well with drinkers— keep multiple drinkers around, and replace the whole thing every day (or oftener, if it needs it). See that the previous day's drinker is thoroughly washed and dried before it is used again— it may not *look* dirty, but it still needs cleaning! Use a good bottle brush for cleaning tube drinkers, and always swab out the insides well, no matter what kind of drinker you use. Keeping the drinking water clean and fresh is one of the best and simplest means to prevent disease.

I prefer not to use the drinker bottles with the steel tube-and-ball tips, as I find that bits of food can get up into them where it is difficult if not impossible to spot and remove. If food gets stuck on the inside and begins to rot, it can be hazardous to your bird's health. Since you can't see such a problem when it occurs, the first you would know about it would be when your canary got sick— and you wouldn't know why.

Variable-sized perches:

You will need at least two variable-sized perches, and one swing, for each 'set' of perches you have for your pet canary's cage. This is so you can easily replace a dirty perch with a clean one at any time you should happen to notice that it needs doing.

Some people will tell you dowels make fine perches

for canaries. This is only half true; if prepared properly, dowels *can* made acceptable perches, as long as a few guidelines are followed. First, never allow the same-sized dowelling to make up 100% of the available perching in the cage. If you *must* use all dowel perches, then you should use at least three different sizes, to allow the bird to stretch and exercise his feet.

Another important step is to prepare the dowels properly– before you allow the bird to use their new perches, get some coarse sand paper, grades 50 or 60 is about right, and firmly scrub every little inch. The idea is to get them rough enough so as to be easy for the bird to grip, without causing splinters. Overly smooth, slippery perches have caused many a sprain.

Clean a wood perch the same way, using coarse sandpaper. Water is a sadly inefficient way to clean bare wood, as any carpenter will tell you!

I like many of the manufactured perches made of tough plastic, shaped so as to provide variable footing. Variable footing is *very* important to maintain the health of your bird's feet– they need to have the opportunity to change the grip of their feet on a regular basis. Some artificial perches are even made to look like wooden branches, and can make an attractive addition to any cage.

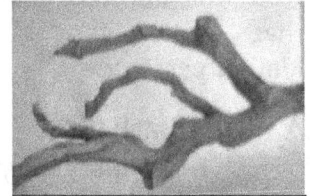

Twist-on perches are useful, and can be either plastic or wood.

Natural branches can make nice perches, too, but must be collected from non-toxic trees that grow well away from any road. Make certain they have not been treated with fertilizers or sprayed with pesticides of any sort.

When you've found a safe tree, select and cut the branches you wish to use, trim off all the leaves, bring the branches into the house and immerse them for a half-hour to an hour in the bathtub in cold water with approximately 5%

chlorine bleach added.

Use bricks or stones to weigh down the branches and hold them under the surface of the water, then leave them to soak until the time is up. When done, rinse thoroughly, and stand them somewhere to air dry for a day or two. I don't recommend using the oven for drying green wood, as the wood will crack and split if dried too fast. These fine cracks can trap toenails, and can also collect and hold food particles, droppings, and bacteria.

One final point, about perches— please, never use sandpaper perch liners on any of your bird's perches. They tend to slip and roll, unbalancing your bird and making it possible he could fall, plus, they will give him sores on his feet. Imagine standing on sharp gravel in bare feet all day— that's what you are asking your bird to do, if you use this kind of perch cover.

A Birdie Bathtub

To a canary, very few activities are as necessary or as pleasurable as a good bath. Many a new canary owner has commented on this, often while staring in a bemused fashion at the droplets of water spread far and wide from their new pet's dedicated ablutions.

Besides being fun, though, bathing is absolutely necessary in order for a canary to maintain his health. It helps keep the feathers clean, and encourages him to spend lots of time preening. This is necessary to maintain proper feather condition.

In turn, preening ensures that the feathers retain their ability to protect and insulate the canary for the full life of each feather. If ever you see a canary whose plumage looks neglected, rough and dull, you will know that you are looking at a sick bird.

He may not *act* sick, particularly if he knows you are watching him— all birds will try to mask symptoms of illness until they are too weak to do otherwise— but his feathers can never lie.

Offer your bird cold water for bathing, in the special 'bay window' type birdie bathtubs made for this purpose. These are designed to hang on the cage door, and will help keep your cage floor from getting soaked every time the bird takes a bath.

Do *not* use the larger tubs made for budgies and other parrot-type birds, and be sure not to use a tub with a mirror in the bottom— very few if any canaries will use such a tub.

Make sure that the water is no more than a half inch deep, and that it is *not* warm. Warm water will strip the feathers of the preen oil necessary to keep the feather in good shape— without it, the feathers soon become dull, dry, brittle, and prone to flaking.

Cold water does the opposite, and actually 'sets' the oil on the feathers, making it easier for the bird to distribute it evenly across the entire feather web, when preening. This helps the feather to stay in good shape for longer.

Floor Coverings

The simplest and best floor covering of all is paper. These days litter beddings are becoming more popular, especially since there seems to be a widespread belief that this type of floor covering does not require daily attention.

In actual fact, this is not the truth. All bird species are highly susceptible to dust, fungus, and mould, and litter beddings based on ingredients such as wood chips, paper, ground walnuts or corn cobs, etc., can provide a wonderful place for such toxins to accumulate, if not tended to daily. It is almost impossible to control the dust such products can produce, and breathing this is bound to shorten the bird's life span even if it doesn't affect his health— but it probably will.

The most serious problem I have heard of associated with these beddings, though, is the danger that your bird might eat some of it, particularly if you use corncob bedding. Even birds who have a steel grating in between them and their bedding have been known to get a hold of pieces of it, and swallow them. Don't ask me how they do it, I just know it happens.

My avian vet has found many a bird, dead of 'mysterious' causes, that has turned out to have a crop stuffed full of corn cob pieces. Once ingested, they absorb water and swell. They do not digest, and will not pass through the crop. Once the bird has eaten enough that its crop is full of this material, there is no more room for food, and the bird slowly starves to death.

All newspaper print in North America these days is required to be non-toxic, and in many cases there is not much problem with smudging anymore, either; using newspaper to line your bird cage no longer means a bird with dirty-looking feet and tail feathers from the ink on the paper rubbing off.

It's not necessary to tediously cut every piece of paper to line the cage with by hand, either. Instead, prepare a stack occasionally, by taking the bottom tray of the cage you need liners for over to your pile of papers ready for cutting. How many sheets you can do at once depends on the thickness of the paper— I find about 8 sheets at a time works well for me.

Align one corner (two sides) of the papers, and plunk your tray on top of the pile, lining up the edge so it hangs over by a very little bit— no more than double the thickness of the material the tray is made of. Hold the tray firmly in the middle, and tear away the excess paper from the other two sides, using the edges of the tray as a guide.

Voila! One neat little pile of paper, suitable to be placed in the bottom of your pet's home. I put a week's worth of papers in at once, then pull off a layer a day. The weekend is when the cage gets a more thorough cleaning anyways— so it doesn't take more than a few seconds to tear a pile of liners for next week.

Cuttlebone/mineral block

Minerals are essential to the maintenance of a bird's health. Grit or gravel, however, is not. It was believed for many years that all birds required small amounts of grit, which was used in a sort of 'pre-stomach' arrangement to help grind and digest the bird's seed. It is now known that this is only true of birds who swallow their seed whole, rather than husking it as canaries and most parrots do.

You can provide a slow digesting 'mineral grit' based on oyster-shell, instead of the indigestible grit usually sold for birds, or if your bird will use them, you can simply provide a cuttlebone and/or a mineral block. Be sure to fix the cuttlebone firmly to the cage, with the softer side facing in.

Kale is usually cheap & easy to find, & provides mega quantities of a variety of essential nutrients.

If you use a lot of eggs in your household, you can save the shells, dry and bake them, and offer these to your birds; similarly to cuttlebone, they are a perfect source of the exact mineral needed by birds for strong bones. Every time you use a raw egg, save the shells. Allow them to air try, and when you have enough to fill a small pan, put them into the oven at 250 degrees Fahrenheit for at least a half an hour. This will kill any bacteria that might be on the shells. Don't be tempted to raise the heat any higher— if you do they can get quite smelly!

When they are completely dry and brittle, remove them from the oven, crunch them up (not too small!) and keep a small cup of them in the cage at all times.

Vitamin supplements

All the minerals in the world are useless without the vitamins necessary to digest them. All indoor birds need a good vitamin supplement in addition to their regular diet – it is next to impossible to provide adequate supplies of vitamins to an indoor bird solely through his diet, no matter how good that diet is. I like to use the dry powdered vitamins meant to be sprinkled lightly on soft foods, rather than using the brands meant to be added to water.

The problem is that canaries don't tend to drink enough water to get much of a dosage when you offer vitamins in the water, and besides, they will begin to break down soon after being added to the water. This encourages slime and bacterial growth, and requires extra cleaning efforts to maintain proper hygiene.

It is, quite simply, both easier and safer to use a good dry vitamin powder, and offer your pet bird a dose once or twice a week on some well-liked food. A small spoonful of cous-cous, cooked rice, or prepared oatmeal is usually quickly gobbled down by canaries, which means you will know your bird got the entire dose; something that just doesn't happen if you offer him vitamins in his water.

The last, and to me most important reason I don't like offering vitamins in water, is that some birds are very suspicious about any changes to their routine, and may refuse to drink enough of that funny-looking-and-tasting water to keep their body functioning properly. Limiting water intake can be very damaging to the kidneys especially, and while you may not notice a problem immediately, such damage can shorten a bird's lifespan by years.

Clean, fresh seed

Last but not least, you need a source of good, clean, fresh seed. Try to find a store which has a good enough turnover of their supplies that you can feel sure that the seed mixes you buy have not been sitting on a shelf for months on end; such mixes will be stale, with lower nutrient levels.

Most of the time, the same criteria applies to the stores which sell bulk seed in bins— after a few days, that seed can get very stale— and usually you will have no way of knowing how long it has been sitting there when you buy it.

Don't be afraid to perform a quick check before you buy, either; fresh seed should taste good, perhaps a little sweet or nutty. For seed that's been bagged in plastic, flip the bag over and check for dust. The more dust, the older the seed. Finally, fresh seed will sprout fairly readily. Canary grass seed should sprout in 7 to 10 days, most other seeds in 3-4 days.

Once you've found a good supply of fresh seed, rather than keeping it at room temperature where it will quickly get old, store your fresh seed in the freezer. An old yogurt tub or small ice cream bucket makes a good storage container, and is easy to get at. Freezing the seed will kill any grain pests or pest eggs that might be present, and keep the seed from aging.

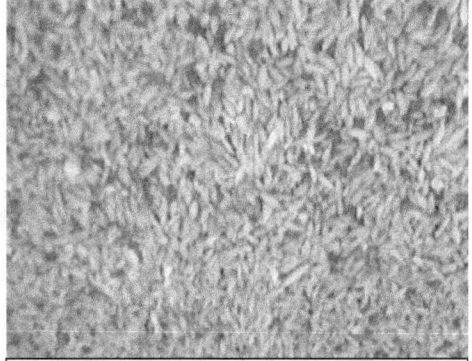

A plain canary mix with 90% canary grass seed; the other 10% is canola, flax, & oat groats. There should be *no* millet!

Frozen seed thaws within minutes, so you will able to simply take out a spoonful of seed a day to refresh the supply in your bird's cup. Be careful to avoid removing the entire container from the freezer and leaving it to sit, for even a few minutes, at room temperature— this will cause condensation on the inside of the container, and can damage the seed, especially if it happens over and over again.

Chapter 3
Finding the Right Canary

Now that you have your cage all set up, you need a canary. But just how do you go about finding the right canary for you? Unfortunately, this is rarely so simple as walking into a pet store.

Most people who want a canary want it for its song. Yet asking at what age a male canary will start singing, is a little like asking when your child will start to talk— the real answer is, it depends! Some start early, some start late— and there is no way of saying if either bird will be a better singer in the long run.

There are many other factors involved too, such as heritage, environment, diet, and more. The amount and kinds of interactions with other creatures around him, whether human, animal, other birds, can also affect his singing; if

One of the author's canaries *(photo by Michael de Freitas).*

he feels that there's nobody around to listen to him and admire his claim of ownership to his territory, he may feel there's no point in bothering to make a claim. That's what singing is all about, for a canary.

It's a good idea to be certain you are buying your canary from a reputable supplier who knows his canaries. Unfortunately, many pet stores do *not* fall into this category. Even fairly good pet stores may not know much about how or where your bird was raised, or under what conditions, yet having this information can prove to be invaluable, especially if you are new to keeping canaries.

Remember, most pet store employees are there to sell the products and stock, not to educate their customers! Some pet stores and people are working to change this, but as of yet they are few and far between. If you know of a good pet store, give them your support— we need to make it very clear that these are the types of places we would like to see more of!

But for now, what this usually means that if you want to be certain your canary comes from a healthy background, and was raised with care, love, and attention to detail rather than in a 'pet mill', you will need to locate a good breeder.

There are several ways to approach this problem. You may be able to contact some breeders through your local avian vet. Any breeder an experienced bird vet is willing to recommend is likely to be well worth your time considering.

Another good method entails locating your local bird clubs, and asking them for recommendations. Whether or not it is specifically a canary club doesn't much matter, as most members will know quite a few of the other 'bird people in their area, no matter what species or breed they happen to keep.

How do you go about finding your local bird club? Depending on how well established they are, and how often they do or don't publicize their events, bird clubs can sometimes be difficult to locate and contact. However these days, even if you don't have the Internet at home, many libraries, community centers and such offer free limited access, and there's always bound to be an Internet Café around which can will allow you to browse the web for an hourly fee.

This will allow you to search for local or international bird club listings— and you might be surprised what it's possible to find! A good place to start is with National organizations, such as the American Federation of Aviculture, or the Avicultural Advancement Council of Canada. Many countries have such organizations, and many have websites that list other national, international, and local bird clubs.

Finally, there's another alternative method for finding just the right canary— go to a bird show, and contact the breeders there. You'll have a chance to look over some of their birds, and often you can make arrangements to visit at their home to choose your bird.

Whether you meet the breeder at a show or bird mart, even if you think they have fantastic birds, I still recommend that if at all possible, you visit the breeder at home before you buy a bird from them. This way you can verify how the birds are raised, and check that his flock is properly care for, and enjoys healthy housing and surroundings. Here's some of what I look for when visiting a breeder's bird-room or aviary with the notion of buying a singer.

A canary hen looking for a good nesting spot examines a lined nestpan for suitability.

Firstly, will he allow you to see the kind of set-up he has? Even if you are not allowed too close to some areas, he should be willing to allow you to give the premises a quick look-see— if not, he could have something to hide, and I would not buy a bird there.

Are all of his birds bright-eyed, tight-feathered, healthy and active, with clean vents, and bright colours? Or are the birds dull, dirty, scraggly-looking, and lethargic? If I see the latter, I don't buy.

What kind of condition are the cages and general

premises in? Canaries, like all birds, can be rather messy, so things can get a little spread around in very few hours— but messy is quite different from just plain dirty. It should be obvious that the premises are cleaned thoroughly on a regular basis.

Another point to watch for is if the breeder is interested in what kind of home you will provide for his youngster, or if he wants you to just buy and go. If he tries to rush you through a sale and out the door, be wary— it's a sign he doesn't much care about how his birds fare in your care. It has been my observation that most good breeders care passionately about the eventual fate of the youngsters they've raised.

The presence of toys is not so common in some birdrooms, but when I see them, the breeder gets a big plus mark. Canaries are quite intelligent for their size, and any kind of stimulation that encourages play is, in my opinion, a healthy and necessary part of their environment, and helps encourage proper development. Most canaries will manage to play even without toys, with whatever they do have— paper, seed, greens, water— but if there's safe toys provided, you'll know the breeder cares about his birds' happiness, as well as their beauty and song.

Something else I always check for is to see if the birds have greens and/or vegetables as well as seed and water. This earns the breeder a big plus too, as feeding greens takes more trouble and time than just tossing some seed in a cup, and is very important for the birds' psychological well being, as well as their general level of health.

Finally – and it always shocks me how many buyers neglect this step, or take assurances that it will happen in lieu of hearing the actual thing— if you want a singing canary, be sure to only buy a bird you have heard sing!

If you haven't heard him sing before you plunk down your money, you are in effect buying a pig in a poke, and could wind up with anything. Sometimes this will work out fine— but sometimes it won't. And what happens if, when he does sing, you don't like his song? This can happen, too.

The trials and tribulations of moving to a new home and a new care system may see him stop singing for a few days, or even a week or two, but if he was singing just before he moved, you will know three things. The first is that he does sing. Besides this, you will know that you like the way he sings, and also that he is healthy enough to regain his song soon.

This last also means that he is healthy enough to adapt relatively easily to a new environment with a minimum of stress and fuss, which might not happen with a canary chosen less carefully.

Keep these ideas in mind when you are looking for a canary for yourself, and odds are that you will come home with a wonderful bird capable of brightening a decade or more of your life. After all, the best pet should make you glad you took the time to find his breeder, and choose him carefully.

Leafy endive is a cultivated relative of the lowly dandelion, and makes a great treat to offer your canaries. As a bonus, it also happens to be very nutritious.

Even better, finding and buying your canary from such a breeder means you will have another great resource available to you; such people rarely mind answering any questions you may come up with, if phrased considerately. Such a resource is invaluable, and can't be measured in terms of dollars and cents.

Chapter 4
Basic Canary Care

Before You Do Anything Else

If you are going to own a bird, you need to know a good avian (bird) veterinarian. Most general vets are quite out of their depth with birds, who are very different from the more commonly kept pets such as cats, dogs, guinea pigs, etc. Please do not even consider consulting one of these vets unless you know for a fact that they also have plenty of experience with birds. To find a good avian vet, consult the member's listings for the Association of Avian Vets. You can find many of them listed online at www.aav.org

Now that you know you will be able to get help if you need it, let's move on to home care.

The Home Cage

Try not to keep a canary in a round cage— it will give him psychological problems by restricting his ability to move naturally.

The ideal canary cage is rectangular and at least forty inches long, fifteen to twenty inches wide and twenty-five or thirty inches tall or more, with bar spacing of no greater than a half inch. Place differently sized perches in parallel at either end. Be sure you do not use too many perches and restrict his flying room— canaries need lots of air space in order to be able to exercise properly by flying.

Rectangular breeding cages often make good pet cages too. This wire cage is being used to house a clutch of recently-weaned young canaries.

Consider training your canary for free flight within a limited area of your home when you are around. It's easier than you might think, and it will add enormously to his well-being, particularly if your cage happens to fall a little short of ideal, as can so easily happen, Patience and consistency are the keys to taming your canary to safely fly free— see Chapter 6 on taming for more about this.

Please don't expect your canary to share his cage. Canaries are *not* socially inclined, and in general do not appreciate company in their cage. Some can learn to get along, but usually they will be happier and sing more if given their own space. Canaries are very territorial by nature, and the less dominant birds will almost always suffer in a shared environment. Probably the biggest cause of premature pet canary death is due to enforced sharing of a cage.

Place your canary's cage carefully, so as to be sure that he has shelter from any drafts, and if it is ever in direct sunlight, be sure that shade will be available too. Look out for windows— placing a cage too close to a window will practically guarantee a draft will be present.

Food and Water

Fresh water must be available at all times! Never let a canary go without water, if he has no water for as little as 16 to 20 hours, he may not survive.

Use a high quality seed mix. The seed should be fresh; the best way to test this is to see if you can sprout a few seeds, just as if you were going to plant them in your garden. Fresh seed should sprout fairly easily. Most seed will begin to sprout within a week or less.

The best seed mixes will contain about 80% to 90% canary grass seed (the beige-coloured, pointy seeds); the rest will be mostly canola (also called rapeseed), a small round black or brownish seed, and some flax (brown shiny pointed seeds). There may be small amounts of teazel or lettuce, but nothing else. Some mixes use the cheaper white millet for filler, but **most canaries cannot eat the larger white or yellow millets, so these should not be present!**

Greens Daily Please!

Fresh greens are a must if you want to have a healthy and happy canary. They are essential to both his physical and psychological well being. Give him a selection each day of what's available for the season, and remember, as long as he is used to eating greenery, he can consume at least half his body weight a day or more.

Some good choices are broccoli, savoy cabbage, kale, or broccoli raba (rapini), mixed with grated carrots. They learn to eat grated carrots faster if you mix them with the chopped greens, and it's a good idea to encourage this, because most pet birds don't get enough vitamin A, and most greens and especially carrots have quite a lot.

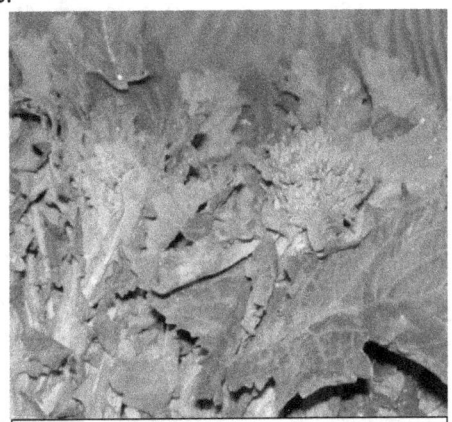

Rapini, also known as broccoli raba, looks a bit like a very leafy broccoli plant, but is more nutritious, and tastes spicier. Canaries adore this power-packed green, so offer lots!

More good choices are dandelions (no pesticides, please!), leafy endives, mustard or collard greens, the Chinese sprouting broccoli known as 'Gai Lan', or any other nutritious leafy green.

Be careful when you are serving any vegetable in the spinach or beet family, not to give too much. This includes beets, chard, spinach, sorrel, and other related vegetables. Small amounts are safest with these vegetables, especially for hens who might be laying eggs, or for birds feeding young chicks. This is because plants in this family contains fairly high levels of oxalic acid, which binds with and prevents the digestion of calcium, so important to the proper development of eggs and bones.

Avoid giving too much lettuce, (except romaine), as it is too watery. You can give fruit such as apple, pear, or orange in limited quantities, but stay away from softer fruits such as peach, papaya or mango, these can make their feces too soft, which can have deadly consequences for a canary.

Treats & Extras

Be very choosy if you must buy store-bought treats such as candied bells, spray millet, moulting, condition or song foods. They are usually stale, and will offer little to no nutrition. Even if you do find some fresh enough to buy, these treat seeds are very fatty and should be given no more than once a week most of the year, and no more than a teaspoon per bird at a time.

Canaries can damage their livers eating too many fatty seeds, so be sparing, even though they love them. I have seen many people give their beloved pet canary a large spoonful per day of one or another of these treat mixes, thinking that since they were using a different treat every day, that this was limiting the bird's intake adequately.

This is *not* a safe practice, and will practically guarantee that the canary fed in such a manner will develop fatty liver disease, kidney or heart troubles in a year or two.

Another important fact is that grit or gravel are **not** a necessity for proper digestion in canaries, who husk their seed when eating it. The only birds who actually *require* grit are birds who swallow their seed whole, such as chickens and pigeons.

A good source of calcium and other minerals *is* necessary to maintain good health, though. Some people provide this through the use of a cuttlebone and/or a mineral block. These work well, but you must make sure that the bird eats them— most will, but some do not.

Others may prefer to offer the supplements known as 'mineralized grit' in a small dish. This kind of product is most often sold as a 'mineralized gravel' mix, and is based on slow-digesting crushed oyster shell, rather than indigestible sand.

You may add baked, sterilized eggshells or crushed cuttlebone or mineral blocks to such a mix if you wish, or do as I do, and simply offer a small cup of baked crushed eggshells on their own, and fix the mineral blocks and cuttlebone (still whole) in the cage. Just save the shells any time you use raw eggs, and dry them in the oven at 250 degrees Fahrenheit for at least an hour, then crumble (not too finely). I always keep some crushed eggshell available in a little cup.

Vitamin supplements are a necessity for a bird who lives indoors. Many brands specify that they should be served mixed with water, but I find this is not a good method with canaries, who, being so small, drink very little. Some will refuse to drink such water at all, which can lead to stress and dehydration problems, or, longer-term, kidney problems.

A homemade 'playpen' for canaries is used to hold a spray millet. Short pieces of natural raffia, hemp, or jute ties add chewing & tugging interest, and can be easily replaced.

My preference is for products designed to be simply sprinkled on the bird's vegetables, fruit, or other such soft foods. As long as they find the flavour acceptable and you don't use too much there is rarely any problem getting them to consume a product like this.

Do please be careful not to offer too much of any such dietary supplement, as it can be as dangerous for your bird as too little. The key to successful supplementation is to use good judgment, and to offer such products in moderation, as a complement to a well-balanced and varied diet, and fortified by regular 'healthy check-ups' with your avian veterinarian.

Keep Your Bird Clean

Change the paper on the cage floor daily, and do a major cleaning of the cage and perches every week. This will help you avoid and prevent diseases and such pests as mites.

Remember please that canaries are particularly sensitive to toxins of all sorts and refrain from using sprays of any sort around them. Perfumes, air fresheners and similar heavily scented products should likewise be banned. When washing their equipment, ensure that all traces of any cleansers are thoroughly rinsed off before returning it to the cage.

Avoid sandpaper perches and flooring, they will only give your canary sores on his feet. Various shapes and sizes of perching are best. Natural branches are fine as long as they are from a non-toxic species and are well washed.

Make sure you never offer your bird perches made of yew, cherry, or cedar wood; all of these may be toxic, particularly if chewed on. Alder, manzanita, apple, aspen, willow, rowan, eucalyptus or birch are all safe choices. Make sure you remove all the buds and leaves and wash and dry the branches thoroughly before offering them to your bird.

The Moult – Feathers Everywhere!

Canaries moult once a year, usually in the mid-to-late summer. You can expect a normal moult to last six to eight weeks or so. You should protect your canary from any unusual stress or major lifestyle changes during the moult as they are much more susceptible to health problems due to sudden changes in routine during this time.

Give your canary extra nutrition and variety in his diet when he is molting. If you have a red canary, now is when you want to make sure there is lots of carotenoids in his diet, to ensure good colour. If you use soak seed and nestling food, (see Chapter 18) this is an excellent conditioner and energy source for a moulting bird, and can be served daily until the moult is over.

Frequent bathing is essential, especially in summer. Make sure that your bird has access to his bath every day during the moult, too, if you can. This is important for the proper growth and unfurling of the new feathers. Frequent bathing is important all the year around, but is a *must* for a moulting canary. Use cold water (***not*** warm!) in a non-slip dish or store-bought bird bath, with the water about a half-inch deep. Give baths early in the day and remove them after about an hour. *Never* let your bird get wet in the evening, as damp feathers at night could make him seriously ill.

This breed is known as the Gloster canary, these two show the dominant mutation usually called a 'crest'
(photo by Michael de Frietas)

Hot or cold drafts from a furnace or an open door or window can make your canary ill if he cannot get out of the breeze. Be watchful for feathers falling out-of-season— they could indicate the presence of an unsuspected draft. Just remember that there must be *some* air circulation. I don't recommend keeping canaries outside; there is too great a chance of exposure to disease from wild birds or mosquitoes.

If your bird moults for a period of twelve weeks or more, be sure to consult with your avian veterinarian, as prolonged moulting is *not* natural and may be an indication of disease or malnutrition. Sometimes, only an avian vet can tell for sure!

A trio of the author's canaries. *(photo by Michael de Freitas)*

Chapter 5

Encouraging Song

One of the most commonly heard questions from new canary owners is, "Why won't my canary *sing*?!?"

The reasons for a canary not singing can vary widely, but depend generally on how comfortable the bird is in his environment, his overall health, and his personality.

This means that it can sometimes take a bit of doing to ferret out the real reason for why any particular canary is not singing— but if you keep trying different ideas, you will be bound to figure it out eventually.

The first thing to do is to check that you have the basics straight. For example, are you sure that the bird is a *male* canary? Many hen canaries can sing quite well, although most are not physically capable of the trademark long trills and warbles of the males. However, some can 'fake' this well enough to fool even an experienced ear— especially when younger. As they get older than a few months, they may stop singing, leaving a pet owner wondering.

Another time when many canaries sing little if at all, is during their annual moult, which normally occurs once a year, in mid-to-late summer. A canary's annual moult should last no more than six to eight weeks— if you find ten or twelve weeks has passed and your canary is still moulting, this could be a sign of illness, and you should contact an avian vet promptly.

Conversely, a bird who does not moult when expected to also may be ill, and should be looked at by an expert. It takes a lot of nutrients to moult, and if they are not available, the bird's body will not be able to support a proper moult.

Sometimes a canary will stop singing (or not start) because he is unhappy or uncomfortable in his environment. This makes it important to check to be sure that you have given him an appropriate cage, set up to accommodate his needs.

Make very sure no drafts are present. An unnoticed draft of either warm or cold air has been the cause of many a canary's loss of song!

Most canaries will not sing as much, if at all, if they are sharing a cage. Canaries are *not* a social species, and don't like company in their cages, outside of breeding season (and sometimes not even then). Most pet canaries require a cage of their own to be really happy.

If you are sure that the above causes do not enter into the picture, then the next thing is to check with an Avian vet.

Sometimes canaries stop singing because they are ill. There may be no other signs present to make you suspect that this may be the case, as canaries, like all other birds, will do their best to look and act normally when they think they are being watched, no matter how ill they are. This will be the case until the bird is too weak to act normally, by which time it may be too late to help him.

So if you suspect that there is a possibility your bird might be ill, it is always wise to check with an expert, rather than try to treat the bird yourself. You could, after all, guess wrong— but if you do, it will be your bird who pays the price.

The Social Factor

Canaries have *much* more capacity for intelligent thought than most people realize. In their native habitat, they are faced with decisions and problems many times a day—where to eat and drink, how to avoid predators, what relations they will have with others creatures both within and outside the flock... all these challenges and more must be met on an everyday basis.

Hundreds of generations of evolution under these conditions has given the canary not only the *capacity* to deal with this amount of stimulation but also the *need* for it.

Traditionally, canaries were kept in small cages. It was believed that a bird who was given too large a cage would spend too much time playing, and not enough time singing.

One of the author's young canaries.
(photo by Michael de Frietas)

It is true that a canary in a small cage will sing a lot, especially at first. Lacking company and room, he will spend all his time announcing his presence to the world. In the wild, this activity would bring other males to challenge his right to be present and hens to be courted and wooed. Wild birds must also learn to deal with the many other species with which they share their world.

In a household environment this simply does not happen. Many canary owners are content to leave him in his cage and rarely interact with him other than when his needs are being attended to.

Canaries are driven by the need to establish and

dominate a territory. His song is an announcement to the world that he is prepared to defend his right to and ownership of his territory to all comers. If he does not feel there is a chance for him to have the right to his own little bit of the world, he is not likely to try to stake his claim.

So how does one go about eliciting a response from a canary who has proven to be healthy and male, but who will not sing?

First the physical environment of the cage must be scrutinized. The area must be free of either warm or cool drafts no matter what the time of year. There should be no frightening objects, large or small, in the area immediately over the cage. Placement should be neither too high nor too low, being ideally just below head height for a human standing next to the cage.

Seed cups and drinkers must be visible and easy to use. Don't use the covered cups unless you know your bird will use them; more than one canary has starved to death because he would not put his head in a little hole to eat. They can concentrate seed dust, too, which is not safe for your bird to breathe.

Perches should be placed well away from food and water dishes so that the seed, water, and vegetables stay clean; this is one of the easiest ways to prevent problems with disease or pests.

The cage should be neither isolated nor in the middle of everything. As with most aspects of life, a happy medium is the ideal. Your bird should be able to see family activity without feeling overwhelmed or threatened by it.

Sunshine is always enjoyed by canaries, but shade *must* be available at all times as well. Anyone who has not seen a canary enjoying a sunbath is in for a real treat!

Home Tweet Home

Next, look at the cage itself and its contents. Is the cage large enough, and appropriately shaped for a canary to use the space? Is it too crowded for the bird? Does it make the bird feel safe and at home, or threatened and exposed?

The traditional round cage is the *last* cage you want to have for a canary. Even a larger round cage will be difficult to adapt to a canary's needs, and because of this it will also tend to get dirty faster and make the bird feel less at home.

Canaries, you see, like most small birds that are adapted for flying rather than climbing, move primarily back and forth. A rectangular cage allows for a perch at either end, so that the bird may move naturally. If the perches are far enough apart, he will be able to fly a little, and get some exercise and fun.

A round cage simply does not allow this. The result is that the canary is deprived of some of his most natural, instinctive movements. This restriction will often produce a bird which feels threatened and/or exposed, although this can be hard to discern unless you have had some practice with canary body language; similar to, and yet in its own way quite different from that used by the psittacine (parrot) families.

One of the author's young canaries.

Because such birds cannot play or move freely, they often become rather badly cage-bound, subject to panic attacks at the slightest change in their environment or routine. This is probably the main source of the common belief that canaries are delicate and sensitive; in actual fact, when cared for properly, the canary is one of the hardiest and most adaptable of all the songbirds.

The ideal (not always attainable but a good goal) cage for a canary will be wider than it is tall, rectangular in shape, forty inches or so long, at least fifteen to twenty inches wide, and twenty-five or more inches tall, with bar spacing of no more than one-half inch. It should have a perch at either end, placed about four inches in from the bars and at about a third of the cage height.

If a swing is to be included, it should be placed so that it does not interfere with the bird's movements between the two fixed perches. Central placement ensures that the cage liner rather than dishes or perches are soiled.

I like to provide a little shelter by way of a light coloured cloth hung across one end of the cage. It is not necessary for this cloth to cover the entire end of the cage as long as it is arranged so that a portion of one of the perches is relatively private.

This mimics the natural shelter that would be available in a tree. While many tree branches are exposed, it is always possible to find a nook shaded by leaves or other branches.

Waterbabies

Water must be available at all times. A canary without access to water will probably not live for more than 24 hours; less if the weather is hot.

Canaries are exceptionally sensitive to traces of undesirable elements in water, so if there is any doubt about the quality of the water source, I may boil and cool the water I use for my canaries, or even buy bottled water for a time. Note that distilled water is not good to use for this purpose, it is missing essential ions and trace minerals found in most drinking water.

Bath time will be greatly appreciated by your canary— I sometimes think my birds act more like they are half fish than all bird— and, if possible, should be offered once a day, in the summertime at least. Please don't let your bird go for any more than two or three days without a bath if you cannot give him one every day.

Put his tub up in the morning, and take it down after an hour or so, to prevent him drinking the used water. This way you can also be sure that his plumage will be dry before evening comes. Wet feathers at lights-out will mean you will have a sick bird on your hands in short order!

The Bread of Life

Seed should be as fresh as possible. Once exposed to air whole seed will go stale quite quickly, much as bread will. If you *must* buy large amounts, try to freeze as much as possible, and remove small amounts as needed. Freezing the seed not only keeps it fresh for far longer than any other method (including refrigeration) it also has the added benefit of killing any insect larvae or eggs which may happen to be present.

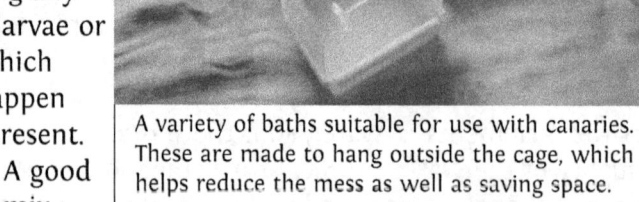

A good canary mix

A variety of baths suitable for use with canaries. These are made to hang outside the cage, which helps reduce the mess as well as saving space.

will contain about 80% canary grass seed. The rest of the mix should be mostly canola and flax. Small amounts of other seeds, such as lettuce, teasel and poppy may be present, but what you should *not* see is the large white or yellow millets. Most canaries cannot crack these larger, harder shelled seeds, but they are often used as filler in the cheaper mixes.

Blow the chaff off the top of the seed in the cup at least once a day if the bird lets it accumulate there; more than one bird has starved to death with a full cup of seed because they will not try to eat what they can't see is there! I have always found that most canaries are not the messy eaters many people seem to believe them to be. Given properly fresh seed, they generally stop throwing it around and settle down to eat it.

Imagine if you will, that you are very hungry and somebody has given you a loaf of stale bread. The best slices will be in the middle of the loaf— would you not eat these first? This is all that many of these canaries are doing; searching through a cup full of stale seed for the fresher-tasting bits.

Oatmeal or oat groats are a valuable addition to a basic canary diet. Most can't eat oats unless they are hulled and crushed or rolled, but once it is served in a form they can handle they devour them with relish. It is similar to canary grass seed in nutritional content, but a little higher in oils.

Oatmeal, rolled oats, or breakfast oats; different names for the same item.

This makes rolled oats a useful diet supplement in cold weather and during the moult, when the bird needs the extra energy. Be aware that, as with most treat seed and song food mixes, too much can make your bird fat and unhealthy. Give any one treat seed no more than once or twice a week unless the bird is weaning, breeding, or moulting, in which case every day is all right, but only for the duration of the condition.

The Energizers

Vitamins and minerals are an absolute necessity for indoor cagebirds. You can offer vitamins the traditional way, via addition to the water, but I try to discourage use of this method for canaries. They are suspicious of any new taste or colour in the water, and will probably not drink enough to do them much good. Also, after the first few hours the vitamins are decomposing and no longer available for digestion. This renders the cups slimy and can make them difficult to clean properly.

I like to offer powdered vitamins sprinkled on their soft foods, such as a soak seed and nestling food mix (see Chapter 18), fruit, veggies, or greens. As long as you don't use too much they will usually devour this with great relish. As an added attraction, some mixes include trace elements and beneficial bacteria and enzymes (probiotics), which can only be for the bird's betterment. If your mix doesn't include probiotics, you can always buy them separately and add them yourself. Again, just be sure not to use too much.

Gravel is *not* necessary in order for a canary to digest his food— although many people believe it is, research has shown that birds who husk the seeds they eat do not require grit to help their food digest. Only such species who swallow their seeds whole, such as chickens and pigeons, rely on the presence of grit in their crop to help them grind and digest their food. A good source of minerals, though, *is* necessary to every living being, and canaries are no exception.

Minerals can be easily provided through access to both a cuttlebone and a mineral block. These may be ignored for months on end, and then suddenly the bird will begin to use them. It is the rare canary indeed who will not at least sometimes use a cuttlebone or mineral block.

Please, Play With Your Food

One of the best toys you can give your canary is a variety of greens or vegetables to chew on. As well as chopping them up and serving mixed in a dish, try being creative and make your bird work a little for his goodies.

Try slices, wedges, or chunks, squeezed through the bars above a perch or wedged into a clip. Use apple, broccoli, corn on the cob (sliced with the cob into round chunks), carrots, beets, or radishes, kohlrabi (a favourite), or any other such similar veggie. Canaries will relish all these foods, once they understand that they *are* food.

Another good way to offer these foods is on a bird skewer. These are sold in pet stores, and come with a nut on the end to hold the food on the skewer, and, incidentally, to prevent any accidents with the sharper end. Most birds I have known love chewing on their own little veggie shish-kabob.

Most people have no idea how much vegetation a canary can consume. Up to fifty or sixty percent of his body weight a day can quite safely consist of vegetables and greens; it is a myth that this can cause diarrhea, except perhaps if the bird has seen no such food for a long time and eats too much. Eating lots of greenery may cause more liquid urates to be produced, but as long as it is not mixed with the feces this is normal, and not a sign of illness.

A mix of organic home-grown canary treats; coarse-grated carrots, mixed with chopped kale, carrot tops, savoy cabbage, nasturtium leaves & rose petals, ready to be served to the author's canaries.

I have never had any problems associated with allowing my birds to eat as much greenery as they like; and I never or rarely encounter many of the problems common to many traditional breeders, who carefully limit the amount of vegetables and greenery their birds have access to. A coincidence? Perhaps, but I myself doubt it!

Forever Green

If you can, offer a dish of chopped greenery at least every other day or so. If you have a Red canary, add lots of grated carrots to his greens every day, to help maintain good feather colour. All canaries, red or not, can benefit from the extra vitamin A they can get from their carrots. This is especially important when he is moulting.

Use nutritious greens such as winter kale, savoy cabbages, romaine lettuce, Italian rapini, leafy endive, culinary dandelion, and other such power-packed greens. A favoured delicacy with my birds is the Chinese sprouting broccoli known as 'Gai Lan'.

Almost any dark leafy green is good, even such things as carrot, turnip, or broccoli leaves. Be aware, though, that some greens, such as spinach, beets, sorrel and chard, can bind with calcium and slow or prevent its digestion. I never serve these greens when I have hens laying eggs, for example.

Remember that canaries are extremely sensitive to chemical pesticides and fertilizers. Because of this I try to ensure that any greens, fruit, or vegetable offered my birds is organically grown, or at least very thoroughly washed.

Most canaries are unabashed and utter pigs about eating anything green. This means that chopped greens are useful for mixing with new or unusually coloured vegetables. When first served grated carrots or other veggies, my birds would not touch them, but when I began serving them mixed with chopped greens they soon got used to them. Now it is more common to see them picking the grated veggies out of the mix to eat first!

Playtime

Simple toys such as hanging chains with beads to slide about are greatly appreciated, as is any toy with interesting things to poke at or tug on. One favourite must be the simplest of all— two or three pieces of natural fiber kitchen twine cut 3 or 4 inches long and tied about a cage wire 2 or 3 inches over a perch, with the ends hanging loose inside the cage. Most canaries will spend quite a lot of time preening and tugging on this kind of 'toy'.

It is my opinion that every canary should always have

a swing. The movement mimics that of the lighter branches at the top of a tree, and they seem to find it relaxing. Most also seem to like the fact that swings must be hung from the roof of the cage. This gives them a high perch from which to oversee household activities.

If your canary ignores his swing, maybe there is not enough room in his cage to allow him to easily jump up onto it— try to ensure that the perches below it are far enough to the side so that he will not have to hop straight up to get onto the swing.

One toy, commonly given to hookbills from small to large that should never be given to a canary is a mirror. These are useful for providing company to a social species, but canaries are *not* social, but rather are highly territorial.

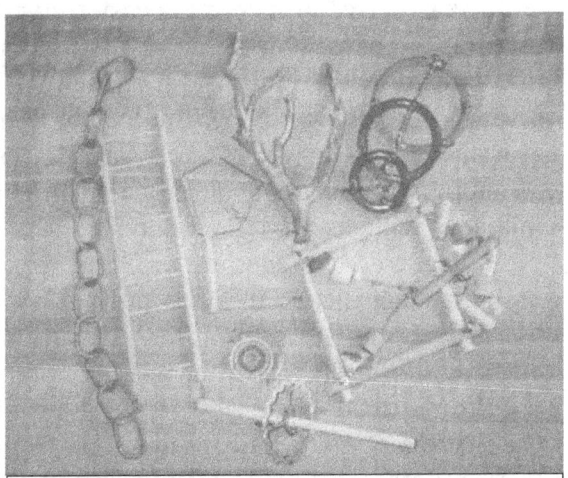

A few of the toys used by the author's canaries. Yes, healthy canaries love to play! Many toys can also offer varied footing, helping keep the feet healthy as well as the bird's mind well occupied.

Depending on the bird and the time of year, he may choose to treat this 'new bird' as a threat and an intruder, or as a potential mate. Either way, the result will be a very frustrated canary. Because of this aspect of their nature, mirrors are irresistible to a canary. This might not sound too bad, but it means that most canaries will spend all their time in front of it, and may forget to eat, drink, or move about enough to stay properly healthy. A situation definitely best avoided!

The Leg You Stand On

Perches are another way to offer variety in a canary's environment. There are many safe kinds to choose from, from the many non-toxic species that can give you natural branches to the huge variety of all shapes and sizes available in the pet stores. I like to keep a larger amount than I am actually using on hand, so that a soiled perch may easily be replaced with a fresh one.

Plastic tree branches are easy to wash and offer as much variety of footing as the real thing. This is very important for the overall health of the foot. Perches that offer a variety of grips allow the foot to exercise and stretch naturally. Make sure that the surfaces do not get too smooth and slippery— an occasional roughing up with a bit of coarse sandpaper will ensure a good non-slip grip.

Real tree branches are nice to have, if you care to go out and collect them, but a few precautions must be observed. You must be absolutely certain that the tree is of a non-toxic species. It should be at least a hundred feet or more away from a road, further if there is a busy highway nearby.

Some of my favourites are apple, mountain ash, alder, aspen, and willow. Curly hazelnut or willow is fun for the birds too! I remove all the leaves and scrub the branches thoroughly with a stiff brush and plenty of soap and water before they ever enter the house.

Then they are given a long soak in the bathtub, in a mixture of cold water with about 5% bleach added. Using cold water means you and your birds can avoid inhaling the dangerous fumes that would be spread through the house if you used hot water— these fumes are not good for either you or your birds!

After a long soak I drain the tub and rinse the branches several times with cold water before a final rinse of scalding hot water to remove the last traces of bleach. The branches are cut to a bit longer than needed and left to dry at room temperature.

I don't like to oven dry wooden perches, as they can split and crack if dried too fast, and those tiny little cracks can catch a toenail and trap your canary faster than you can say "*kazaam*". It never seems to happen when you're looking, either!

Rope perches are okay, but care must be taken that the bird's nails are kept trimmed, so as not to catch on the fibers. For the same reason, the rope must be replaced *immediately* once it begins to fray.

The Moult

Normally, most canaries will moult, that is, replace their feathers once a year, usually in the heat of the summer. This period should last about six to eight weeks or so; if your canary is throwing feathers for longer than that, see an avian vet, as he may have a problem— prolonged moulting is *not* normal.

You will find that your canary will be less energetic than usual when moulting, and he probably will not sing much, if at all. He will greatly appreciate any extra coddling you can throw his way in the form of extra-nutritious treats, an extra-reliable schedule, a predictable environment, and lots of seed, vegetables, and greens. Soaked seed with nestling food (see Chapter 18) is a particularly good source of nutrition during the moult.

Try to protect your canary from extra stress when he

The posture indicates fear and stress; this canary is afraid of something nearby.   (*photo by Hans Classen*)

is moulting, as sudden shocks to a moulting bird can lead to feather loss over large areas of the skin. They may take longer than usual to begin to regrow, and in the meantime you will have a half-naked bird, vulnerable to every stray draft and breeze that comes along.

Your Feathered Child

Let your canary know that he is a member of your household. Speak to him every day. See that he has some form of interaction with all the members of your household, even if it's only pausing near his cage to speak to him occasionally.

Gaze gently at your bird when you're nearby, and always speak or make some small noise or other. A predator will approach silently and will usually be staring at his prey—so such an approach will make any canary very nervous, and understandably so!

Sound is important to any creature evolved in a forested environment, and they should never be kept in too quiet an area. To all birds, silence means just one thing—there's a predator nearby!

This is the *only* time you will ever hear silence in any forest. Many canary owners will leave a radio playing near their bird when they are not home; this assures him that he has not been left at the mercy of an unseen predator stalking him from somewhere within a silent house.

Although independent by nature, all canaries live within the larger framework and social order of their flock. Anyone who wishes to have a happy, healthy, singing canary must convince the bird that he is able to establish a place for himself within his human flock.

Having accomplished this successfully, you are liable to find yourself possessed of such a lively, vibrant little songster that you just may find other people asking *you* to help them with the question *"Why won't my canary sing?"*

Robirda with two of her pet birds; these two are society finches, who can also be tamed using the same methods she uses for taming canaries.

Chapter 6
Taming Your Canary

To my mind there are very few creatures on God's green earth as sweet-natured, beautiful, unassuming, and as easy to keep as the pet canary. Very few other creatures will eat but a teaspoon or so of seed a day, plus a little greens or fruit, that will yet sing their heart out for you, and still be as easy to care for.

However, many people seem to think that they are difficult to keep, or, having acquired one, find that they have a lot of trouble discovering just what these pretty little members of the finch family need in order to thrive.

For those poor souls who wish to find some information on how to tame them, well, let's just say that there's not much to be had. Information on breeding canaries is only a little easier to find, and very often training, taming and keeping end up being done largely by trial and error, with widely varying degrees of success.

These days, pet canaries are not as common as they once were. Ever eager to try something new, John Q. Public has gone hunting for a more exotic pet, and somewhere in all this the canary quietly began its fade into the background of the pet trade.

Too many pet shops these days carry little or nothing in the way of quality canary supplies, and in most cases this quite accurately reflects the trade, for the small merchant has little choice but to follow the demands of his customers.

To my mind, many canary breeders have, all unwittingly, played a part in the decline of the canary as a favoured pet by focusing most of their attention on breeding and showing, to the exclusion of all other facets of the trade.

What am I talking about? Well, for example, consider the desires and goals of a show-bird breeder. He looks over his chicks, but he cannot properly tell when they are young if they will become the bird he's been trying to breed or not. He almost always wishes to wait at least until his birds have grown their first set of adult feathers before thinking about selling any of them.

The young birds are kept in large flights with others of their age, which is great for muscle development but does very little to accustom them to a friendly human presence. Any contact with humankind is generally brief and quite impersonal, either at feeding-and-cleaning time, or else when being administered medicine or some such.

Soon they will be put in a rigorous round of show training, and if they are good enough, an even more strenuous round of shows. It is often only after the shows are over and the next breeding season is drawing near that the birds are again sorted, and the ones that will not be needed for breeding are sold.

At this point they rarely are what I would call a good pet canary. Their habits of interaction with their own and human kind are ingrained into them with the force of constant repetition. Time and again I have been told by people who own or have owned one of these birds that canaries are difficult to tame, and that all they are good for is to sit in a cage and sing.

While it is true that canaries do this extremely well, that is in no way the limit of their potential. The canary has an amazing capacity to learn, if given the chance, and is so far the only creature known to science that has been proven to be able to regenerate its brain cells, thus enormously increasing its capacity to learn in relation to its brain size and complexity.

The fact is, it is much easier to tame a canary when it is younger, before it has formed a solid opinion of the world. I believe that breeders who refuse to sell any of their birds as pets before nine months of age to prospective pet owners are, in the long run, cutting the throat of the Canary Fancy.

Beautiful as they are, many people find a bird who does nothing *but* sit in a cage and sing boring, especially when that bird adamantly refuses all advances of friendship. And who could blame him, after having gone through the trials described above?

To a bird like this, people are anything but potential pals, and although they may make superb breeding stock, it is rare for one of these birds to become a good pet.

When choosing a young bird you wish to tame, it is important to observe the entire group you are choosing from for awhile, in order to be able to determine each bird's personality. An easy method I have used involves getting a handful of a treat you know they love, such as fresh young dandelion leaves, or a handful of leaf lettuce. Put your hand into the cage, holding the greens so that they are easily visible to the birds, and watch their reactions closely.

Most of the youngsters will flock off to the far end of the cage, and will either be frantically trying to escape, or else peering suspiciously at you. Often, though, there will be the odd bird or two who will instead approach quite closely, studying you and the treat in much the same way you are studying them.

This trait of studying the situation is the one you want to see in a bird you want to train. A canary who has this attitude will often practically train itself, being eager to elicit the desired response from you (in this case, access to those yummy greens).

I find that it helps to work with only one canary at a time, away from any other birds. Too often they serve only to distract him. You want his attention to be focused on you and you alone while you are working with him. Always move slowly and calmly, letting him see what you are doing, and don't expect too much out of him at one time.

Several short sessions are always preferable to one long one, as if he gets tired or over-stressed, he'll forget everything he's just learned. His actions will tell you a large part of what he is feeling; tightly sleeked down feathers and an open beak (like a dog pants) means *stress! fear!* If you see these or similar reactions, stop immediately and let the bird rest for a short while.

I like to leave a *tiny* bit of the treat behind in the cage at this point, to encourage him to draw the conclusion that some good can come out interacting with people. You want to give him just a taste, so that he always wants more.

As time goes on, he will begin to look forward to your training sessions, at first just to get it over with and get to the treat-eating part, but eventually he will learn to enjoy your company— especially if you make it clear to him that making friends with you will be the only way he will ever get any more than a tiny bit of his favourite treat.

You want to initiate more of a conditioning process in

many ways, rather than the more direct training you might give a dog or child. Let him get to feel familiar with his surroundings, and always reward him with a tiny bit of a treat when he performs as you wish. **NEVER EVER CHASE HIM!** He *must* come to you willingly, even if you must lure him there.

Positive rather than negative reinforcement is crucial. If you keep a regular routine and always train at the same time of the day you will find he will quickly get used to the whole thing and will anticipate his session with you, eager to 'train' his human to provide him with all those fun things to do and goodies to eat.

As you have probably realized by now, canaries are creatures of habit, and once a routine is established, they rarely break it, unless something drastic happens to shock them out of it. I can't emphasize too strongly the importance of positive

Robirda working with a young canary

reinforcement in establishing the routines you wish your bird to learn. This is the basis on which the success or failure of your training attempts will hinge.

If you're patient and persistent, your reward will be a sweeter miracle than you could ever expect; the trust of a tiny, feathered scrap of life, with a personality as vivid as his song is beautiful. In order to ensure that you know what I'm talking about I'd like to paint you this mental picture.

It's evening, and you are returning home after another day's work. As you approach the house you hear your canary trilling along with the radio, left on low volume to keep him company. As you enter, he warbles his delight at seeing you, and bounces over to the door of his cage, waiting for you to come over and say hello. He hops eagerly onto your hand as you open his cage door, and flits up to your shoulder to exchange 'kisses'.

You check his seed and water and then go about your evening routines. He supervises all this with great interest from his vantage point on your shoulder, occasionally leaving his perch to steal a nibble of this or that, but mostly just singing sweet merry nothings into your ear.

He has his dinner while you eat, and afterward you relax together in the living room and play together awhile. Always, whatever he does, one eye is on you and what you're doing, and his play is as centered around pleasing you as it is himself. He knows when it is bedtime, and returns to his 'house' by himself, perhaps even flying back out to scold you if you're a little late putting his cover on.

Sound too good to be true? Well, I know it's possible, because it's a similar routine to the one my first pet canary and I developed over the years we spent together. It was a surprisingly warm and affectionate relationship, much more so than I would have ever imagined as possible prior to having him in my life, and even though he has been gone for several years now, I still miss him terribly.

Although I have trained other canaries, and helped still others to learn to train their people, I will never forget the lessons he taught me about what a *real* pet canary can be capable of.

* * * * * * * * *

So now that you've decided to handtame your canary, just where do you start?

There are a couple of things you should check right away. First, do you know how old your bird is? If you have bought your canary from a pet store, there is no reliable way to know his age unless he carries what is known as 'closed band', a steel ring on his leg.

Usually these bands will show the initials of the club that issued them and the year they were issued, as well as an individual band number. Sometimes they even carry the breeder's initials. Many breeders use these bands to prove the year of hatching.

Why should you check his age? For the simple reason that, if you really want a truly tame canary, you should start with as young a bird as possible. A canary six weeks to six months of age will be *much* easier to convince that you want to be his pal.

Darker canaries are often overlooked as pets, being considered dull and sparrow-like; but they can be very personable, and many sing very well indeed, often better than the more popular yellow, white, or red canaries.

Of course, it is more difficult to tell if you are getting a male canary when the chicks are so young, but never mind that— canary hens make nice pets too! As a matter of fact, over the years, many of my favourite birds have been canary hens.

Unlike many species, whether or not a canary has been hand-fed will not make much of a difference in how tame he becomes. The canary's social development does not depend on how he is fed, but rather on his interactions with those in the world around him.

This development occurs particularly quickly between the time the young bird fledges, and the time it has finished moulting into its adult feathers, at approximately sixteen to twenty weeks of age— interaction at this age will usually result in a tame canary, whether it was hand-fed or not.

Too, canaries are quite capable of making up their own minds who they will be friendly with— just because a canary is friendly and tame with one person, does not mean he will be tame with another.

Any breeder can usually help you to acquire a young bird suitable for taming, but before you start, just one more thing. Take him to an avian vet to make sure he is healthy. (Please, do *not* go to a regular vet who says, oh yes, I do birds too!)

An avian vet specializes in treating birds and exotic animals and will be able to give you a clean bill of health more accurately and probably more cheaply. Now that you are assured that he is healthy and young you can proceed.

I suppose that there are many ways of handtaming canaries, but I have found a few facts that have helped my efforts in this direction enormously. The main key to success is the resolve to be persistent and consistent. Patience helps a *lot*!

The best of these methods is based as much if not more on a canary's psychology as it is technique, and can usually be hastened along with the judicial application of a few favoured treats to sweeten the dish.

Canaries, you see, are a member of the finch family, and, with them, share some basic actions and responses to different situations.

For example, a typically seen response to aggression from another bird sees the attacked bird remove himself from the area to the opposite (usually) side of the cage or flight, where some vigorous beak-whetting takes place. Finch psychologists say that this is a form of displaced aggression. Taking his anger out on the perch instead of another bird preserves the flock's health and well-being.

Another response is typical when nervous and confused. When startled, many finches will panic, and try to escape as far away as possible as soon as possible. Others will freeze. Sometimes the freeze response will segue into flight, but the most common response is nervousness.

At this stage, they recognize the intrusion of an alien but so far non-threatening object(s) into their lives. Their lack of comfort with this affair is shown by a restless hopping back and forth. This is in order to keep the metabolism active in case the situation should change and sudden flight be required.

The answer to handtaming a canary, then, is simple. You are bound to make him nervous anyway, so you might as well take advantage of understanding his responses.

This canary is feeling extremely nervous, as indicated by the gaping mouth and highly tense posture. *(photo by Hans Classen)*

First, decide on your schedule, and keep to it. A reliable and predictable pattern to his life will help your canary keep steady, enabling him to learn his lessons faster and more thoroughly. One or two training sessions of about ten or fifteen minutes each per day should be adequate.

Remove your bird and his cage from their usual surroundings. Then calmly remove all food from the cage, and all perches but one. I find it helps if I make a point of never giving any bird I want to tame any sort of treat outside of taming times; keep their diet regular, adequate but bland.

If the bird panics at the sudden changes, let it settle for a few minutes and regain its equilibrium. Then, place a treat you know your bird likes in between the tips of your fingers, and put your hand in the cage, lining up your hand so that the edge of your hand makes an obvious perch, with that enticing bit of lettuce or apple or whatever at one end of it. (I usually use lettuce- most canaries are absolutely piggy about a tender leafy type green.)

The bird should calm down fairly quickly. If it doesn't, and stands on the perch or hangs off the wire of the cage side 'panting', almost like a dog, this is a sign of stress. If this occurs at any time you are working with a bird, immediately stop everything you are doing and go away for a few minutes, just long enough for the bird to recover. Leave a *tiny* bit of the treat you were holding in your fingers behind in the cage, to help teach the bird that good things can happen when things look scary too.

If all goes well and you have carefully blocked off all means of escape from the cage, including any gaps around the space you are putting your hand through, (a desperate-to-escape canary can squeeze through some mighty small spaces!) you will soon have your bird where you want him. That is, in a small area, with only two perches available to him; his own, and your hand.

The drive to hop back and forth will soon have him restless, and sooner or later, if you are patient, he will 'accidentally' land on your hand in his restlessness. Chances are he will pop right back off again, so fast you'd think he'd been scalded, but from that point on you are almost home free.

I find that you can usually almost see the thought processes going through their little heads once you are at this part. They've been hopping around for a few minutes now, with nary a bite of food (birds in the finch family eat a *lot*) and there's that yummy looking piece of lettuce just over there making matters worse.

"Gee, but it'd be grand to get a bite of that...but that *hand* is over there, too...on the other hand, (foot?) I was just over there and nothing happened...maybe if I'm *real quick* I can sneak a fast munch on the way by..." and after a few minutes of this they generally manage to 'talk' themselves into giving it a try.

I like to accompany all this with a steady stream of low murmuring comments, it really doesn't matter what you say, the idea is to provide a soothing background type of noise. This lets the bird know that it is safe... to a species that evolved in a forest, silence is anything but golden! The *only* time it is quiet in a forest is when there is a predator around. Sudden silence will always put a canary on guard, *not* the effect you want to have!.

So there you are, standing there murmuring to a bird cage, when all of a sudden it happens, and the bird lands on your hand and starts to munch on whatever you are holding. What do you do?

This canary is alert but curious, and is not feeling at all afraid, a good state of mind to be in if you're working on taming him.   (photo by Hans Classen)

Well, the first thing you *don't* do is move; not even the teeniest bit. If he gets the notion that a hand is an unstable perch, it'll take him a good long while to unlearn it. You want him to come to the conclusion that a hand is a nice safe place to stand.

The first time in particular, just hold still, even if it tickles. Let him decide for himself that it's time to 'park' on the other perch before you move your hand in the slightest. Then S-L-O-W-L-Y remove your hand from the cage, get another little bit of a treat, put it in the cage, replace his food and water, return the cage and bird to their usual location, and *then* you can sit back and heave that big sigh!

Getting him to recognize your hand as an okay place to sit is the worst hurdle in handtaming a canary. Once you're over that, it is just a matter of slowly accustoming him to the routines you want him to learn. 'Cue' words can help, too; they should be short (one or two syllables) and distinctive enough sounding that the bird can easily recognize them.

For example, one canary I trained was a very forward-moving, aggressive little bird. All his motions were vigorous and bold, and he never held back. He would jump onto my hand so hard that you'd hear a little 'plop' when he landed, and the phrase 'plop-plop' sort of snuck into those comforting little murmurings that I mentioned earlier.

A few days later he was acting distracted, didn't show much interest in his taming session, and without thinking I said something along the lines of "Come on, little plops," and to my extreme surprise he hopped forward the instant he heard the word 'plop'. Hearing that word every time he'd bounced over to my hand to snag a bite of lettuce had conditioned him to associate the action with the word, so when he heard the word, the action was automatically included in his response!

Once he's used to sitting on your hand, and knows that it also brings food and water into the cage at your direction (most small birds tend to see the hand as a separate being, different from the face that looks into their cages) then you can begin to accustom him to sitting on a moving hand.

Begin by slowly moving your hand towards the other perch in the cage. If he hops off when you begin to move, fine; slowly let your hand drift back to its 'other perch' position and wait for him to come back.

Eventually he'll sit still for this; then slowly move your hand so that it is a tad lower than the other perch, and right next to it. Say your 'cue' word that you've picked for getting him to hop onto your hand, and begin to slowly lower your hand.

If he didn't hop off when he heard the cue word when the other perch was at his chest level, he almost surely will as your hand slowly drops and the other perch comes close to head level. Canaries and many other finches are nervous about having anything closely over their heads; the instinct is to get on top of whatever it is.

Once he is on the other perch, bring your hand up to his chest, hold it just in front of him and repeat your cue word. If he

A tame canary hen perches confidently on her owner's hand *(photo by J. Johnson)*

doesn't hop up immediately, very lightly bump his lower chest with your finger. Once he is back on your hand, drift it back to your 'other perch' position and let him munch on a treat. Keep repeating this exercise over a few days until he is moving easily and on command on and off of your hand.

Only once he is entirely familiar with and comfortable with moving on and off your hand, may you begin to accustom him to being brought out of the cage while sitting on your hand. You may teach him to sit on your shoulder using a similar process, but it is not advisable to let him get used to sitting on your head. You may walk under something and forget to allow for the extra clearance!

Never forget that a house is full of dangers for a small bird. It is your responsibility to check any room you allow your bird to fly free in for any dangers, and eliminate or circumvent them. Canaries are quite capable of learning what is and what is not allowed, but it is up to you to keep an eye on them whenever they are out of their cages.

Please try to remember that even though he is quite intelligent, and has become tame and responsive to you, a canary is full of curiosity, and cannot be trusted to be out and about in your home when you are not nearby and keeping an eye on things. Like many children, pet canaries are endlessly curious— anything and everything is liable to end up in their mouths, and it is just as liable to be something dangerous for him, as not. Limit his freedom to those times when you can be nearby, so you may enjoy your time together for many years to come.

So, there you are. Assuming that you began with a young, healthy bird, you should begin to see results fairly soon. Make sure you always use patience, moving slowly and calmly, letting the bird see what you are doing. Never surprise him if you can help it and always reward him when he deserves it. Lure him to you if you must, but be sure you *never* chase him, so that he will never learn to see you in any other way but as his friend, pal, and provider.

I am willing to guarantee you that if you follow all these steps faithfully, you will soon be the proud possessor of a tame, bratty, bossy, loving, funny, inventive, curious, 'helpful', endearing, adorable, and all-round *cute* little canary. And I know that once you have lived with and been 'owned' by one of these birds, you too will join those of us who love to be heard singing the Praises of the Pet Canary!

Chapter 7

Health and the Avian Vet
By Sharon Klueber

In these days of swift economic change, it can be so important to keep on top of expenses... if we're not careful, it doesn't take long for things to get out of hand!

But while we are keeping tight control of the expenses in our lives, it is wise to also spend a little time thinking about the things we do spend our money on, and what kind of value we get for our dollars.

To my mind, there are very few resources available to any bird owner, whether they keep only one pet, or breed hundreds of birds a year, as valuable as a good avian vet.

One of the author's canaries.
(photo by Michael de Freitas)

I just lost my old-timer Kermit, a canary, after taking him to the vet's a few days ago. I am waiting for the results of a necropsy, so I can learn what he died of.

After a thorough examination when I brought him in, they kept him at the vet's office to take x-rays in an attempt to determine what was wrong with him, take what small amount of blood they could for blood work to be targeted hopefully by what the x-rays showed, and medicate him once they were able to determine what might be wrong.

This is a vast improvement over when I took my first canary to a vet just two years ago. While the vet at that time did physically examine him, the diagnosis was basically a shrug and sending me home with an antibiotic. So obviously some progress is being made!

While there is a bit more information available for treating parrots, there is by and large not a lot of experience or knowledge out there regarding the smaller birds such as budgies, lovebirds, finches and canaries. I suspect a large part of that is due to the fact that these birds cost so much less than some of the parrots that the economics for many folks say it is less expensive to replace a sick bird than to spend the amount it could end up costing you if you have it treated at the vet's.

I can't help but think that there is something missing from that picture... and my guess is, it's not quite what you're thinking!

The fact is that until we as small pet bird owners start indicating that we want to be able to have knowledgeable and affordable treatment available for our birds and taking them to our vets for treatment so that our avian vets can have hands on experience working with them, I imagine that this situation will not improve.

After all, it is basically a world of supply and demand out there— and if we don't demand the care, the veterinary hospitals and clinics won't supply it.

In a small community like the one I live in, a vet who has an interest in treating birds and other exotics (yes, our birds are considered exotic pets along with ferrets, hedgehogs, rabbits, reptiles, amphibians, and the like) also has to treat dogs and cats. In fact dogs and cats most likely make up the largest number of his or her patients.

In that light, it is important if we ever want to have the same level of care available for our birds that is available for our selves, our dogs and our cats, that we bite the bullet and spend the money to take our birds to see the vet when they get sick.

It hasn't always been easy to get good treatment even for our dogs and cats, as some of us will recall. When I was a child the family dog and cat were only taken into the vet for a rabies shot or in the event of an emergency. Far fewer folks spayed or neutered in those days and the diagnostic skills were nowhere near the level they are today.

We as pet owners demonstrated a need for better routine, maintenance care, and diagnostics for our beloved pets. As more and more people brought their dogs and cats in for routine care our vets got more hands-on experience, more data became available, and better, more affordable care was the result. We as pet owners are in a large part responsible for this because we demanded these services.

This melanin mutation is usually known as an 'agate' canary. *(photo by Hans Classen)*

Will it cost as much or possibly more to take your bird to the vet's than it would to buy a new bird? Yes, probably. Will you still stand the chance of losing your bird even if you take it to the vets? Yes, but you will obviously improve his odds of survival by getting him the attention and expert care sick birds so often need.

My pets are family to me— I am close to them, and losing their company is like losing any other family member—

it hurts. At least for me, I find that I can more easily deal with the loss by knowing I have done everything I could for my pet.

I also like to think that even if my bird does die, that the vet will have learned from the experience and may be able to help the next sad little pet finch, canary, lovebird or budgie that someone brings him to be treated, because of what he learned by treating my bird.

I find it frustrating, and I imagine many others do as well, to not have the same level of diagnostic care and treatments available for my birds that I have come to expect and even take for granted for my dogs and cats.

Our veterinary clinics and hospitals are there to provide services to our pets. Dogs and cats have always been popular, and support for their care is well established. But birds are now the third most popular pets, worldwide, and many of those birds are inexpensive to buy.

Price aside, does each life not have as much intrinsic value as any other? I feel very strongly that no life should ever be thrown away lightly, no matter its supposed value.

As for Kermit? The necropsy showed that he had bled out into his stomach. According to my vet, normally that alone would lead to a diagnosis of metal toxicity. The neurological signs he was exhibiting, including twitching, disorientation, and balance problems, along with the x-ray which showed very clearly a piece of metal in the lower end of his crop, makes the diagnosis of metal toxicity definite in my vet's opinion.

Interestingly, Kermit's lungs were clear and all of his other organs looked fine. There was no indication of any type of infectious disease. They never did find the piece of metal. It was described to me as being about a third the size of a canary seed. This would make finding it rather like looking for a needle in a haystack, so I cannot say that I am surprised that they didn't find it.

While I did get a reason for what happened to Kermit

I also got more questions from the test results. Questions that will most likely go unanswered. For example: How long was that metal in his system? Where on earth did it come from? It was small enough I am guessing it could have come in with something I gave him to eat— but I will never know for sure.

While I will definitely miss Kermit, gentle old bird that he was, I have some satisfaction in knowing what it was that killed him and in being able to provide my vet with the opportunity to perform a necropsy on a small bird like a canary. In this case I wasn't charged for the necropsy and I did get a definitive answer.

When my canary 'Blue' died earlier this year and a necropsy was done by a different vet, which I did pay for, I did not get a conclusive answer. It is always a possibility that a necropsy will not be able to show exactly what went wrong, but if we don't try, we will never find out anything— positive or not.

If we don't take our small birds into our vets to be treated, if we don't request necropsies when we lose them, if we don't indicate by doing this that there is in fact a need out here for these types of services and diagnostic skills for our small pet birds, then we will never have them available.

The choice is easy for me. What about you?

Peacock kale and nasturtiums in the author's gardens. Organically grown greens can help to keep your canaries healthy and happy too.

A canary hen works on building her nest.

Chapter 8
To Breed or Not to Breed?

Whether you intend to breed your canaries or not, sometimes it just happens. Canary hens, even when kept alone, will lay eggs in the proper season, if they are healthy, and if there is a male around in condition to fertilize them for her, he just might be happy to do it!

Yet so many pet canary owners decide that they want to deliberately try to breed their beloved birds, and have nothing but problems. Why does this happen? In actual fact, although many sources will tell you that canaries are 'easy-breeding', this is only by comparison to the rest of their close relatives, the carduelan finches.

Most of these birds (including canaries of course) *can* be bred in captivity, but it can be tricky to complete the entire cycle from nesting to weaning smoothly and without problems. To achieve this requires a thorough understanding of the birds' habits, needs and expectations, along with the willingness to do the work involved— anybody who breeds their canaries will do a lot more food preparation, record keeping and cage cleaning than pet keepers ever will!

Especially when new to keeping canaries, many pet owners erroneously believe that a pet canary needs the company of his own kind. Some will then decide that keeping a pair of canaries will best suit their purpose. The two birds are ensconced in a pet-sized cage in the middle of the family living room, and expected to live in harmony throughout the year.

On occasion, if the cage provided is large enough, set up properly, and the birds like each other, this may even occur. But more often, it does not.

Besides the personality of each individual bird, which can be a major deciding factor, in general a canary, whether male or female, tends to be a rather independent-natured, solitude-loving little bird.

Rather than being extremely social, as are most of the avian species commonly kept as pets, wild or uncaged canaries will tend to stake out their own territory throughout the year, and defend it from all intruders. Canary hens can be a little more socially inclined than the males, but (as with so many generalizations) this is not always the case. And even socially inclined canary hens can get *very* territorial when they are breeding.

A male given the freedom to choose will pick his territory, and try to attract a mate or mates to it. Yes, that's right– the canary *hen* chooses the male she is willing to accept, not the reverse. Once she has chosen her mate, she will move into his territory during the breeding season and build her nest there, in return for his protection and aid with her young.

He will defend his territory from all other comers the most fiercely during the breeding season, but in general he will maintain and defend his private territory throughout the year, although that defense may get a little lackadaisical during the summer moult.

A flock of canaries with an adequate amount of room available to them tend to like to flock together while feeding much of the year, and though they may squabble a fair bit, usually it is relatively amiable.

The rest of the time most prefer to go about their own affairs in their own areas. In a small pet cage, many of which are actually too small even for a single canary, there just isn't room for this sort of interaction, and no private space at all is available.

Keeping multiple canaries in small cages is probably the largest cause of premature pet canary death. But if the birds survive this, then the pet owner, who was in actual fact just trying to be kind to their birds, may suddenly find himself or herself becoming a surprised breeder.

Although many don't realize it at the time, this scenario does not have to occur. It *is* possible to keep a single male canary happy, without any other company than you and your family. Given an adequate diet and a proper sized cage, some such family canaries have been known to live for up to 20 years or more!

This mosaic (or dimorphic) canary lacks the facial blaze sported by males of this feather type, so it must be a hen.   *(photo by Hans Classen)*

Breeding greatly shortens the average lifespan of a canary, for hens to around five or six years or so, and for the males to maybe six or seven years. This is due to the high cost in energy expenditure and general systemic stress that the process of breeding— especially feeding the young— puts a canary's body through.

If you have been surprised by birds you did not plan

to have breed, or have a pet hen and just want to keep her happy, you can practice 'canary contraception' by allowing her to lay her eggs, then switching them for the small plastic fake canary eggs sold by pet supply dealers. She can sit on these as long as she likes, and nothing at all will hatch.

If she has not been mated, her eggs will be infertile, however, it's not a bad idea to switch to the plastic eggs anyways, to prevent cases of accidental breakage. Besides, the fake eggs will not lose weight as they age, as will a real egg. This lightening of weight of the real eggs will be noticed by the hen, and her instincts will prompt her to throw them out and lay more.

This often means that she will happily sett for longer on the fake eggs than she would her own infertile eggs, giving you a chance to allow her system to rest and catch up with itself. Keep an eye peeled, however— if an egg she considers fertile still does not hatch after prolonged setting, eventually she will abandon it and lay more.

If you decide that you *do* want to breed her, you should be well prepared beforehand. At the very minimum, for one pair you will need a small cage for the male, a larger flight cage for the hen and any youngsters your pair produce, and a double or triple breeding cage for your pair to breed in.

Remember too, that you will most likely not be able to sell any of the youngsters until they are fully adult, at around six to nine months of age, so plan to have plenty of cage space available for them, and remember to plan for the cost of feeding and maintaining them.

Watching canaries go through the breeding process can be a wonderful education for children— canaries obligingly use open nestpans that are quite simple to see into, unlike the dark, closed boxes so many species prefer. All the action is right there, and can be fairly easily seen.

If you want this experience for your children, you must instruct them very carefully in how to watch the birds without focusing a fixed stare on them, and not to approach too closely, or move too fast when around them. All these actions could make a parent bird feel unsafe, which could cause them to sit too tightly on the babies, thinking they are guarding them from danger, instead of feeding them.

A canary chick, being so very tiny, cannot survive long without being fed. If a canary parent feels threatened enough, she may allow her babies to die of hunger, rather than feeding them. This may seem cruel, but is an instinct necessary for survival in the cruel world of the wild songbird. Canaries evolved this instinct to help ensure species survival, and many generations of living with humans isn't likely to change it.

Some canary hens, particularly if they are used to you and trust you, won't mind you watching them caring for their babies. Most, though, will resent being watched, and if they catch you at it, will refuse to care for their babies while you are around.

Sometimes looking at things sideways can help you figure out just what you're looking at; or at least that's what this young canary belonging to the author seems to be thinking!

This has caused trouble for many a new breeder. Eager to be sure of the new chicks' survival, they hover around the cage, waiting to see if the hen is feeding or not. Very often they don't realize that especially on the first day or two, a canary chick is so small that a hen can easily feed it without looking much like she is doing anything. There is a very good reason for her to feed like this, too, other than to keep you from seeing her feed her babies, that is.

In the wild, tender new hatchlings are on the 'top 10'

list of tasty treats for predators. The canary hen is geared by Nature to watch for this, and if she thinks you begin to act unusually just about the time her babies hatch, she is liable to decide that you want to eat them. That being the case, she will do everything possible to prevent your seeing them.

This chain of events has led to the death of many a new hatchling, but if you are prepared, it is easy to prevent. Simply remember that you *must* appear unconcerned when around a hen with new hatchlings. Be careful not to do anything too unusual, compared to your normal routine, and don't give the birds any more obvious attention than what they are already used to getting. Establishing a routine and keeping to it will do more to sooth a nervous hen than almost anything else you could do.

If you should happen to see the babies, go ahead and look— but make sure you talk 'baby talk' in a small high voice to them, as so many mothers of so many species do when adoring children, their own or another's. This is an easily understood cross-species signal that will tell her plainly that you like her chicks and would never dream of being a threat to them, helping her to relax accordingly.

If you are doing everything possible and the hen still seems nervous and unwilling to feed, check the babies' crops and make sure that they have not been fed 'on the sly'. The crop, is a sort of a 'pre-stomach', and runs down side of the neck. A baby that has been fed will have a thick yellow 'vein' running down the side of his neck, which may bulge quite a lot when the chick gets a little older.

This is *not* a sudden illness, or an unnatural growth, as many a nervous new breeder has been known to think, but is just the baby's crop with some food in it. Far from being a sign of something wrong, it is a sign that everything is going well! The colour can change depending on what the baby is being fed— greens, for example, will look dark green or black, and seeds or portions of seeds can be easily visible. But most nestling foods or egg foods look rather yellow.

If you've checked and the crops are empty, then perhaps the hen is afraid of the male. New mothers in particular can feel this way sometimes, and again, the solution is quite simple— especially if you are using a proper canary breeding cage. Simply use the wire divider these cages come with, and divide the cage in two, leaving her on one side, and the male on the other.

If you don't have a divided cage, open the cage door and allow him to fly out. It's best not to attempt to catch him in an undivided cage, as you might upset the hen. It's easier to let him come out and then catch him outside the cage. Make sure she can easily see him, wherever you settle him, and be sure he can't reach her babies.

Give each has his or her own source of food and water, and see that she has

A view inside one of the author's flights, showing two toys loved by her canaries, a simple set of rings that can be poked at and tugged.

plenty of variety, to tempt her to eat. She will still be able to see the male, but he will not be able to pester her. In a day or two, when she is more used to her new babies and is feeding well, he can be allowed to return to help feed the babies, as long as she is agreeable.

When you are properly prepared, and have a healthy, well-established and confident pair of birds, raising canaries can be a joy and a privilege. The miracle of their growth from the tiny scraps of flesh that hatch out into a beautiful canary within a few short weeks is nothing short of amazing, no matter how many times you see it.

So once you are sure that you want to breed your birds, be sure to make that bit of extra effort ahead of time, and your birds will repay you in more ways than you will be ever be able to count.

Chapter 9
So, You Want To Breed, eh?

Okay. You've decided you want to breed your birds. So, now what? Where to start first? How do you go about finding out what you need to know?

Here's a few thoughts to keep in mind about how to proceed.

Research Your Resources

Your best resource will always be your ability to research a subject. It will be well worth your while to spend a little time developing this skill— it will prove itself invaluable in all facets of your life, over the years.

When it comes to breeding *any* species of bird, even if you can't find any books on breeding that particular species, you can still learn a *lot* about them by learning about the environment their species evolved in and

Chickweed, bane of many gardeners, is a reliable food plant for many of the wild species in North America, & is greatly enjoyed by canaries too.

with. Find out exactly where on the globe the birds you are dealing with came from, then find out what the seasons are like there. Look at the annual daylengths and temperature variations, and note the cyclic variations of weather and climate, both daily and seasonal, averages as well as extremes.

Once you have a fairly good grasp on seasonal climate and the environmental conditions the birds evolved in, look at what types of plants grow there. Find out what foods would tend to be available for the birds to eat, and which would be most available at what time of the year. Also look at what other kinds of birds, animals, or insects share the environment, and as much as possible try to find out how they interact.

Another great resource for learning about breeding your birds is bird clubs. If you don't belong to one already, find one and join it! Experienced breeders can be one of the most invaluable resources of all to a new birdkeeper— if anybody will have experienced the problems you are likely to trip over, it's them. If you can't find a club to join, keep hunting. They *are* out there!

Remember, though, when asking other club members to speak with you about their birds, to be polite. Above all, don't demand too much of their time. If they offer, that's one thing— but anybody who has baby birds at home is liable to be very short on free time. Demanding rather than requesting help can easily garner resentment and withdrawal, rather than the sharing you wish to encourage.

Common sense will always be your best yardstick, and should be applied to any advice you are given. No matter where you hear or read it, search out all sides of a topic, and just as carefully apply it to your local situation. Good advice for the warm humidity of Florida may be completely wrong for the cool humidity of the Pacific Northwest. After all, in the end it is you and your birds who will have to live with your decisions, not anybody else!

Talk to everybody you can find who has any experience they are willing to offer you. Write letters or e-mails if there's nobody local to you. The idea is to learn as much as possible from those who have already had the experience. Remember, though, that they don't *owe* you any of this advice or insight— it is up to you to convince them that you are worthy of their time and confidence.

Take what you can learn about each various method as you find out about them, and analyze them with respect to your situation. Ask yourself what you think you would have done in such-and-such a situation, which actions you would have done similarly, or whether you think a different approach might work better. Then, rather than just trying your ideas, try to find out if anybody has already tried something similar for themselves. Then, *talk* to them about it!

Remember, the more you can learn ahead of time, the better off you will be once you proceed.

Watch and Learn

When, finally, you feel that you have exhausted your resources (or the birds get tired of waiting for you and begin to breed on their own), it is time to remember that the birds themselves are your best source of information. Learn your birds' body language, so you can understand

One of the author's older canaries at nine years.
(photo by Michael de Freitas)

if they are comfortable or tense, when, and why. Use what you know of the environment they evolved in to help you imagine what to provide them to make them more comfortable.

The happier and more secure they feel in their environment, the more inclined they will be to breed, and the higher your success rates will be.

One thing about watching— don't let yourself stare! A fixed stare is the exclusive trademark of the predator in a wild environment, and will instinctively cause great discomfort to any prey species. It may be seen as a challenge by larger species, which can provoke a defensive reaction— so often taken by a puzzled human as "an unprovoked attack".

From the point of view of a creature who evolved as a prey species, being stared at is plenty of provocation. The immediate response will be an impulse towards either fight or flight, provoked by the 'fear' reaction. This is true of wild or wild-caught birds especially, but even hand-tame birds can be very protective of their privacy when breeding. Either way you will not be regarded as a desirable or benevolent presence if you make a habit of staring fixedly at your birds.

Learn to be aware of what your body language is telling the birds, from their point of view. Once you understand how they tend to see things, you will learn to use posture, language, and how you move to impress on them the fact that they are safe around you.

In general, my usual approach is something like this. I adopt an observation post lower than the habitat of the birds I want to observe. I go directly there without looking at the birds, and settle myself. I try to move slowly, and calmly, but not sneakily, and I deliberately make some noise, such as talking quietly to myself.

In the process of getting settled, I allow myself to glance at the birds, but make sure that my gaze travels over them, rather than stopping at them and then passing on. I try to keep my attitude casual, and my body and voice relaxed and calm.

Once in my area, I begin to pretend I am another bird, and 'forage' little bits of invisible nothing from the floor at my feet, occasionally pretending to eat something I've found. In the process I allow my gaze to travel over the birds I am watching, never allowing my eyes to fix on them, but still generally looking in their direction.

I will pretend to preen my hair or clothes occasionally, take small sips of my coffee, and perhaps even read a few lines of a book or magazine between glances. With all this going on, the birds will eventually realize— if they haven't already— that you are no threat to them, and will relax and begin to act normally around you.

This will allow you to observe their intimate behavior, and notice small details about their interactions with each other. If you want to be a successful breeder, it is important to know your birds well, so as to be able to establish compatible pairs. Just like people, each bird has his or her own distinct personality, and this can affect their breedability.

Music To Their Ears

Another widely used technique to help birds relax is the use of a radio or TV. An often-cited reason for this is that it amuses the birds. Perhaps, but it also gives them another important message. In almost every wild environment on the planet, silence is associated with the presence of a predator.

A class of canaries at a show in Vancouver, BC.
(photo by Albert Varda)

A typical forest is quite noisy by day. But if any of the inhabitants should spot a known or suspected predator, they will give a single short, sharp call. Instantly every creature within hearing range of that call will freeze, hunting with all their senses to learn where the predator is.

To a creature with this instinct, noise means safety, and so we commonly find birds who love to talk when their owners do, their volume rising to equal the level of their surroundings. I have seen this instinct lead to some quite funny scenarios, the birds loudly 'doing their thing' to the bemusement of their loving but very puzzled people.

One thing to remember about TV's though— there is some evidence that the rapidly flickering light of a television could cause some damage to a bird's eyes, particularly the smaller species, or a bird close to a television or who has little other bright light in its environment. Because of this, it's a good idea to see that there's plenty of other light sources if your birds can see your TV, and try to keep them as far away from it as possible, whether behind it or in front.

The Air We Breathe

Birds are extremely sensitive to environmental poisons. For them, clean air is not just something nice to breathe occasionally— it can literally mean the difference between life and death.

Birds have *air sacs* instead of lungs. These air sacs have no psilia, such as we humans have in our nostrils and lungs, to act as filters and catch small particles, fumes, and pests out of the air as they are breathing it. Because of this they are very susceptible to problems and ill health due to poor air quality. Many houses can become dusty and dry, particularly when sealed during extreme weather, and the birds living in such houses can suffer as a result.

One tool I rely on to keep dust and dirt on the floors where it can wait for clean-up rather than floating about in the air where the birds and I can breathe it, is a negative ionizer. This is simply a little needle of iron or steel, sometimes found in its own fixture but more often included in an arrangement with a fan and air filter, that is used to generate negative ions.

These negatively-charged ions bond with any dust particles they encounter in the air, increasing their weight and causing them to settle to the nearest surface. If you have ever smelled the air after the passing of a thunderstorm, all clean and fresh-smelling, you already know what air heavy with negatively charged ions smells like. As a bonus, both humans and birds find breathing air with plenty of negative ions to be both relaxing and invigorating.

Cleanliness is a must, of course, but be very aware of which cleaners you use, & how. Common household bleach can cause irritating fumes when used with hot water, for example. If you find you must use some strong chemical or other, be sure and remove the birds from the vicinity to prevent any exposure, and allow ample time for the air to clear before returning them to the area. Better yet, refuse to allow yourself to say 'must', and find an alternative. The range and scope of non-toxic cleaners available is growing every day.

This is a Gloster canary. Since a crest is a dominant mutation, a plainhead Gloster such as this one must be used to breed with a crested bird such as the one shown on page 174 to create more crested Gloster canaries.   *(photo by Michael de Freitas)*

So now perhaps you have a few more ideas to try out. Have fun and learn from your birds, and when you figure out some more good tricks, don't forget to share them with the rest of us!

A tall flight for hens next to a stack of dividable box breeding cages.

Chapter 10
Preparing For Breeding Season

Fall is the time of year when most canary owners are busy enjoying their bird's songs, glad that the moult is over. Some are preparing their young birds for shows, or happily attending them, learning more about the various breeds and species or just enjoying seeing and hearing all the variety of breeds often present at such shows.

Few people are thinking about the next breeding season just then— that is a long way off, with months to go, for those who keep canaries. Often even those who keep species that are not seasonal breeders are not thinking of new babies in the flock just then. Birds that don't breed seasonally are known as 'opportunistic' breeders; their instinct to breed responds to specific environmental conditions. Normally fall weather won't trigger much of a breeding response for eventhese species.

But the truth is that how your canaries are cared for during the fall, can and definitely will affect your breeding season. It will be the results of the care given during the fall that will in due time see a canary owner asking (or not) that so-often-heard question; "Why won't my canaries *breed!?*"

Several months before you want canary breeding season to start is actually the time when you need to begin paying close attention to the canaries you will be keeping for breeding. With fall being such a busy time for so many of us, too often the birds will be put into a cage, (some larger, some smaller), fed and watered every day, and the papers changed daily or every other day— and that's about it.

Other than this minimal attention, it is very easy to not spend much time watching your canaries, especially if you are busy. But if you want to encourage a good breeding season, spending time watching them is just exactly what you want to be doing.

Many breeders like to keep their canaries in larger flight cages or even aviaries, outside of the breeding season. They get lots of exercise this way, and are expected to grow healthy and strong. But if the aviary is not set up properly to accommodate its inhabitants, exactly the opposite can occur.

One of the first things to look at is the interactions going on between various birds. Are there a lot of noisy arguments? Then perhaps the cage is too crowded— you may need to add some perches and/or seedcups, and you may need to remove some of the inhabitants to another cage, too.

A common problem with shared flight cages is the lack of enough perching space. Especially with birds such as canaries, who are highly territorial, this is *very* important.

There should be *at least* a foot or so of perching space available for each bird in the flight. If you see a lot of arguing over who is going to sit where, and for how long— especially during the middle of the day— then chances are that you have too many birds in the cage for the amount of perching space that you have provided. If not, then perhaps you have placed the perches incorrectly.

One high perch and several lower ones, for example, will often lead to a great number of arguments in an aviary—everybody will want to sit on the highest perch. Placing several long perches at the same height will often help to allay such a problem. Don't forget to include some lower perches too, these are also necessary, as one of the ways a less-dominant bird will try to avoid harassment is by making use of these low perches. Do try to make sure that they are placed so as to avoid droppings from above.

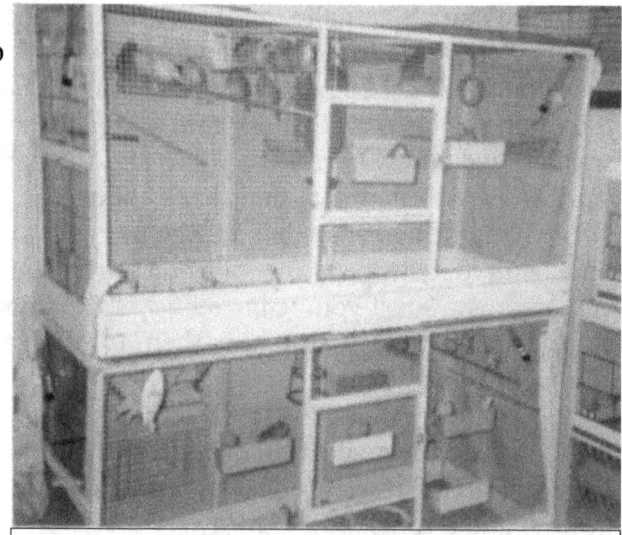

A stack of homemade flight cages in the author's birdroom. Note the many feedcups & drinkers, spaced well apart; this is important when keeping multiple canaries in the same cage, even during the winter.

Another often over-looked factor in successful breeding results, and a very good reason to see that your hens at least are allowed access to large flight cages or even an aviary during the winter, is the amount of flight time the birds manage to get in over the winter months. Particularly for smaller species like the canary, this can literally mean the difference between life and death, especially for the hens.

These tiny birds lay huge eggs, when compared to their overall body size; on average, four canary eggs will weigh close to the same as the hen who laid them. It takes a lot of muscle to force such a relatively huge item from their bodies, and to do this they use the strongest muscles in their bodies. These muscles run the length of their body, beginning at the keel bone and running lengthwise along the skeleton towards the tail. The exact same muscles power their wings when they are in flight.

Adequate flight time will therefore mean a strong, healthy hen, who with a proper diet should have no problem laying her eggs, when the time comes.

Important as it is for the hens, adequate flight time can make a big difference in the male canary's ability to successfully fertilize eggs, too. Sufficient flight time to develop his aerial skill and control, which in turn will mean that he will have developed the power and agility necessary to hover over the hen for that critical moment of split-second timing which successful fertilization requires.

The benefits of plenty of flight time are generally obvious almost immediately— the birds will tend to be happier, healthier, more active, and more resistant to all sorts of problems, when compared with canaries kept in smaller cages.

I can't tell you how many times this has been remarked on to me, often in a surprised manner. The fact is that this positive physical response is usually *so* obvious that even a relatively inexperienced eye can note the difference.

Properly controlled lighting is very important to those species of birds that are photosensitive. The canary is a species that shows dramatic differences in its physical reactions to the environment it is in, depending on the intensity and timing of the lighting it is exposed to. Successful breeding requires a basic understanding of the canary, and for most breeders that includes implementing a well-balanced system of lighting.

Canaries have a nervous system that responds to the changing lengths of the day throughout their year, allowing their bodies to physically respond to the demands of the season. To a canary, breeding season starts when the days have been short, and then begin to gradually lengthen; this signal begins changes to their entire system, causing their body to begin preparing. Successful breeding occurs within two or three months after this beginning.

Confusion occurs when a canary is moved from one system of caretaking to another, especially one on a different lighting schedule. Varying days and nights are responsible for many puzzled queries as to just why the birds are trying to breed *now*, and not *then* (or the opposite). The answer, "Because they think it's spring" often just serves to confuse even more— after all, one glance out the window would tell anyone the season!

But canaries don't think like us. They have evolved with their own ways, habits, instincts, and reasoning powers, that will be applied whether we are aware of it or not.

A plain swing is turned into a great canary toy by simply tying short twists of untreated raffia to the wire. You could also use jute or hemp, but not cotton, as the fibers are too fine.

It is up to us, if we want to learn to successfully be able to care for our canaries, to learn how to understand them.

The long and the short of it is that it's the birds themselves who will, in the long run, be counted among your best teachers. So try to grant them a small part of your attention every day, and simply watch their interactions. Watch what they do, and try to understand why they do it.

Put yourself 'in their shoes', as it were, and you may find yourself becoming ever more entranced with the beauty and complexity of this wondrously interactive, continuously evolving dance which Nature— and your canaries!— will present to your wondering eyes.

Chapter 11
Seasons and the Canary

More than any other factor influencing how the canary reacts to his environment, is one issue. It lies at the heart of any canary's physical system, whether breeder or pet. It influences how he acts and looks, and when he sleeps or wakes. It is a major part of what a canary is, and yet most people don't realize it's there at all.

I am speaking of a trait known as *'photosensitivity'*.

Canaries are very strongly photosensitive. They evolved so that their bodies respond physically to the amount of light which enters their eyes. This triggers the beginnings or endings to some extreme physical changes, which can affect his personality, his health, his appearance, his attitude and even the length of his life.

It used to be that keeping canaries was a fairly reliable project. A pet canary would sing all year long, except for six to eight weeks during the summer when he was moulting. Breeders knew just when in the spring they could expect their birds to want their nests, and there would be time for only two nests before it was time for the moult.

That was before the advent of artificial lighting. Nowadays, canaries are only predictable if all they are seeing is natural daylight, or lights which are on only during the day. That can be a big *if*, too! To a canary, the lengthening days of spring signal the start of breeding season.

Canary breeders who have their birds producing eggs and/or chicks at other times of the year, have used artificial lighting in the birds' quarters to make their daytime longer. This makes them react as if the season is more advanced than it actually is.

Many breeders deliberately do this to get a jump on the season. However my own experience has shown me that this does not give quite the advantage you might expect. Clutches laid earlier in the season often have more infertile eggs than is usually seen in nests from later in the season. I have also found that in the long run, more often than not the better birds will be those who hatched mid-season or later.

One of the biggest problems for most newcomers to breeding canaries is learning to understand that their birds literally react physically to the length of the days they are experiencing.

People are also photosensitive, if to a rather minor degree by comparison. Still, each winter will bring new cases of the disease known as SAD, that is, Seasonal Affective Disorder. This is a kind of depression that has been tied, in humans, to a lack of sufficient natural light.

Most of us don't tend to think much about any of this, though— we are too busy! Many of us think nothing of hopping up in the middle of the night and flipping on the lights, to jot down a note or finish a task. The fact is, though, that if your canaries see this light, it will stimulate them physically, the same way daylight does.

Their bodies react as if it is suddenly dawn. Their internal 'clocks' are triggered, and this begins the series of physical changes that go with the day *and* the season in which days of that length occur.

For a look at the annual changes in the Canary Islands where canaries originated, check the chart at the end of this chapter. Canaries *are* adaptable to extremes outside that range, to a certain degree, but I find this chart useful, in that it shows me the variations of the lengths of the days and nights that the canary species evolved with.

Some canaries are never allowed to complete these annual changes comfortably and in their own time, but are instead physically pushed into suddenly beginning or ending them at the whim of their human family's convenience.

This is *very* stressful for a canary, and over a long term, can lead to health problems, and a much shorter lifespan than otherwise might be seen.

Every year, many canaries are tricked into thinking it is spring when the holiday season comes along and suddenly there is more light and longer days, due to their human family's increased holiday socialization.

Every year I hear of 'surprise' Christmas hatchlings, and every year, I hear of some of them dying. Too often this is because once the holiday season is over, the house lights return to more normal timing, and suddenly the canaries find they are experiencing shorter days once again.

Aggression between canaries can cause serious problems, when they're housed together. *(photo by Michael de Freitas)*

To a canary, shortening days means that the summer solstice has passed, and winter is on its way. This is a signal to all canaries to get those feathers replaced and renewed, *fast*, before the fall weather arrives and the climate becomes more changeable and less reliable. In other words, it's the signal to begin the annual moult.. This kind of stimulation can cause a canary to go into an out-of-season moult, as if midsummer had just passed. Usually this also means that parent canaries will stop feeding any babies still in the nest.

Over the years this kind of scenario has caused a lot of trouble for those new to breeding canaries. The only way out is to learn to understand the effect lighting has on a canary. Once you have lived with them for a few years and watched the incredible annual changes they go through, it becomes easier to understand how important these changes are to a canary, as well as how completely this stimulus acts on them, both physically and mentally.

Perhaps the biggest hurdle newcomers to breeding canaries must learn, is that if they are to successfully keep their canaries healthy, fit, singing and productive, their convenience has to play second fiddle to their canaries' needs.

Creative minds can easily find ways to get around such limits as when lights need to be on or off, using such handy items as extra-heavy cage covers, or, as many breeders do, a separate birdroom where even full houselights won't bother sleeping canaries.

The fact still remains that such accommodation has to be a standard consideration for those interested in keeping their canaries happy and healthy, *especially* if you want them to breed reliably. This applies whether the goal is to have a few pet songsters, or a large flock of show quality stock.

Two other factors that in my experience have quite a lot to do with how canaries react to seasonal changes of lighting and environment are heat, and attitude.

The warmer the ambient temperature, the more amenable your canaries are likely to be towards attempting to breed. As for mental attitude, it has been my experience that this can definitely play a role, too.

Most canaries tend to be quite intelligent, rather more so that you might expect of such a small bird, and some canary hens in particular can take sudden notions. (Many men will insist this is a trait all females share).

In my experience, some hens adore the idea of babies, and think of them year round. At the slightest sign that it might be getting close to breeding season, they will be busily trying to build a nest, and trolling for a response from the males around them. Other hens couldn't give a flit, and breed only when their bodies physically force them to.

My conclusion is that while they may all have similar bodies, each and every canary is as much an individual as any human. We humans are all physically similar too— but that has never stopped each of us from being unique in our own special way. My observations suggest that this is equally true of all of the creatures who share this planet with us.

On the next page you will find a chart showing sunrise and sunset times in two-week intervals over the period of a year in the Canary Islands, which you can use as a guide for your canary's days and nights. If you want to learn to be a successful canary keeper, understanding the concepts behind your birds' photosensitivity and seasonality will have a lot to do with the kinds of results you achieve.

Like many of us, you will probably find that applying this schedule or one similar to it, will be a great help in getting to your goal, by making it possible to predict and understand just what your birds will be doing at any given point throughout the year. Other factors are involved, of course, but most take a back seat to the impact seasonality and photosensitivity have on our canaries.

Remember, too, that if you plan to sell any of the youngsters you breed as pets, that you will need to take a little time to be sure the buyer understands the whole idea of how much his house lighting can affect his canary. He or she won't have to stick *exactly* to such a schedule to keep a pet canary healthy and happy— but staying as close as possible will help any pet canary to have much better overall health, improving both the quality of his life and, yes, the length of his lifespan.

Date	Lights On	Daylength	Lights Off
Jan 1	7:56 am	10 hours, 24 minutes	6:20 pm
Jan 15	7:57 am	10 hours, 34 minutes	6:31 pm
Jan 29	7:53 am	10 hours, 52 minutes	6:42 pm
Feb 12	7:44 am	11 hours, 9 minutes	6:53 pm
Feb 26	7:32 am	11 hours, 34 minutes	7:02 pm
Mar 12	7:17 am	11 hours, 54 minutes	7:11 pm
Mar 26	7:01 am	12 hours, 18 minutes	7:19 pm
Apr 9	6:45 am	12 hours, 41 minutes	7:26 pm
Apr 23	6:31 am	13 hours, 3 minutes	7:34 pm
May 7	6:19 am	13 hours, 23 minutes	7:42 pm
May 21	6:11 am	13 hours, 39 minutes	7:50 pm
June 4	6:07 am	13 hours, 50 minutes	7:57 pm
June 18	6:08 am	13 hours, 55 minutes	8:03 pm
July 2	6:12 am	13 hours, 52 minutes	8:04 pm
July 16	6:18 am	13 hours, 44 minutes	8:02 pm
July 30	6:25 am	13 hours, 30 minutes	7:55 pm
Aug 14	6:34 am	13 hours, 9 minutes	7:43 pm
Aug 28	6:41 am	12 hours, 50 minutes	7:29 pm
Sept 12	6:48 am	12 hours, 24 minutes	7:12 pm
Sept 26	6:54 am	12 hours, 2 minutes	6:56 pm
Oct 10	7:02 am	11 hours, 38 minutes	6:40 pm
Oct 24	7:10 am	11 hours, 16 minutes	6:26 pm
Nov 8	7:20 am	10 hours, 55 minutes	6:15 pm
Nov 22	7:31 am	10 hours, 39 minutes	6:09 pm
Dec 6	7:42 am	10 hours, 26 minutes	6:09 pm
Dec 20	7:51 am	10 hours, 22 minutes	6:13 pm

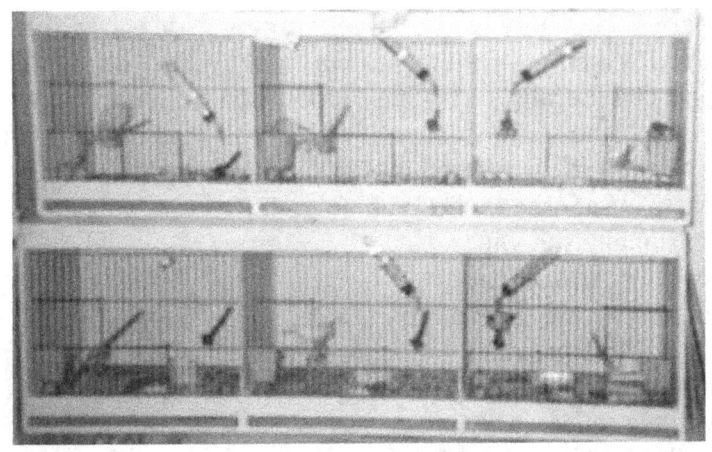

A pair of triple-breeder box cages. Some come with both solid and wire dividers, which is very handy; the wire dividers are used for introducing potential mates to each other, while the solid dividers can be used to make three small cages; remove them all and you have one long cage.

Chapter 12
The Breeding Cage

You can actually use just about any cage to breed canaries in, as long as it is large enough and the bars are not spaced too far apart. But there's a very good reason why you can find cages made especially for breeding canaries— they make your job a *lot* easier, when used the way they were designed.

Canary breeding cages can be found in all shapes, sizes, widths and heights, but the better ones all share one element in common; they can be divided.

Most can be divided into two sections— a few three. Often the better ones are designed to be stacked, and some will even interlock with each other to give you a fairly stable stack. This is a useful design element to have, especially if you plan to breed several pairs or more.

The one essential element to all of these cages is that you are able to easily separate the birds whenever you like without being required to handle or chase them. Since canaries are highly territorial and can be very aggressive, especially during breeding season, being able to quickly divide a pair can literally save a life on occasion.

Without a divider, you will be required to catch one of the two birds up and remove it from the cage. This can greatly upset a hen who is about to lay eggs in a day or two. Occasionally she will become so upset that a problem with egg-binding results. This provides another good reason to use dividable cages— and an excellent reason to avoid upsetting your hens whenever possible.

Most dividable cages come with wire dividers. A few come with both wire or solid dividers, which can be swapped out as needed, so the breeder can choose which to use, depending on his or her needs. This can be a very useful option to have.

Two different box breeding cages, a double breeder and a triple breeder. Note the blanket on top, used for covering the cage fronts at night.

Many pet-style breeding cages are designed as if they were a true double-compartment breeding cage, but with a reduced length. A two-part cage of 24 inches long, when divided, allows each resident only 12 inches of room. This, in my opinion, is not even close to adequate for a canary. A double breeder cage for canaries should be at least 30 to 36 inches in width, so the separate compartments, though only 15 to 18 inches wide, will be useable for the short term if needed.

Another drawback to many pet style breeding cages is that their dividers often require insertion from the top rather than the front of the cage. This prevents any stacking of cages, which can be a greater drawback than you may think. Even if you will only be breeding one pair, you will be better off buying a model that can be stacked. After all, any chicks you produce will need to be kept until they are almost adult if you want to know if they are singers or not, even if you plan to sell them. That in turn means that they will need cages too, once they are weaned.

Traditionally, triple compartment cages are designed for use with two hens, one each at either end of the cage, with a male in the middle section. The male is run with one hen or the other, depending on how the dividers are placed.

Generally each hen is left to raise her chicks alone, in such an arrangement, and the male is kept separately when he is not actually mating a hen. (This is because a male who bonds to a particular female will usually not want to mate with another hen in that season).

While this can and does work well for some people, I find that this one small compartment can get *very* crowded, especially when the chicks are weaning. Often the hen will want to begin another nest before the chicks are fully weaned, but there is no room for any such arrangement in limited quarters. Even worse, frustrated hens may decide to begin using the soft young feathers their chicks are growing in, and begin plucking their chicks for feathers to use refurbishing her old nest.

With the male in the central compartment and another hen in the far end, there is no alternative but to leave such chicks in with their mother until they are fully weaned. By then they could be plucked almost bald! This can be *very* hard on a youngster, forcing his body to spend far more energy on regrowing feathers than it normally would.

I tend to use triple breeders in a slightly different way. I allow each hen the run of two compartments, and keep her male behind a wire divider in the third. When they have accepted each other, the pair is allowed the run of all three sections. With the nest at one end of the cage, this allows the male some room for activity that will not necessarily involve his pestering the hen, as can happen in smaller cages.

When the chicks hatch, there is lots of room to put out a wide variety of foods. This is one of the most useful parts of such an arrangement, as in my experience the broader the variety of nutritious foods presented to them, the better the parents will feed their chicks.

Because he is not being used with two hens, the male is more likely to be a reliable parent, and feed his chicks. If so, then you will have a built-in solution if the hen decides she wants to build another nest before the chicks are fully weaned— simply give her a new nest in the far end of the cage, and allow 'Daddy' to take care of weaning the young.

Even if she must be kept behind a divider to limit her gathering of nesting material to those you provide, there will still be plenty of room for the youngsters and their father in two compartments, while the hen 'rules the roost' in the third.

In such cases I will remove the divider for a short time in the morning to allow the pair to mate; then it is replaced, and she has her peace and quiet for the rest of the day. I find this approach a far more adaptable use of triple-breeding cages than the traditional one, and it has made triple-breeders my favourite choice for a breeding cage.

A 'birds eye view' of a half-built canary nest in the author's birdroom.

Chapter 13
Nests & Nest Liners

If you are going to be raising canaries, you need a good solid nestpan, one easy to attach to and remove from the cage. It needs to sit solidly, in place not bounce too much when a bird lands on it, and it must sit level, without much of a slant.

You never know when you will need to inspect the eggs or the chicks, and it is easier to do this if you can just lift out the entire nestpan; fumbling about in a nest with your hand at an awkward angle is one of the best ways I can think of to accidentally break a delicate canary egg, or even worse, to accidentally hurt a tiny chick.

So make life easy for yourself, and make sure when you set the nest up that it is easy to reach from the cage door, and see that you will be able to remove it easily any time you like, without bouncing the contents about.

For the same reason, it's helpful if the style of nest you choose has a flat bottom, so that if you should happen to be candling eggs or banding chicks, you will be able to place the nest on the table without worrying about tipping out its inhabitants. Don't worry if you can't find any flat-bottomed nestpans though; you can always wash out a few tuna tins and keep those handy to act as holders for a round-bottom nests. Just place an empty clean tin on the table, and park the nest on top. The tin will support the sides of the nest enough to keep it from tipping over, and is wide enough to keep it fairly stable, even if the chicks are shifting about some.

Contrary to what you might think, a canary hen's favourite spot to build a nest is rarely if ever likely to be in the darkest corner of the cage, the one you and I would consider to be the most protected.

Instead, she is more likely to choose one of the brighter spots in the cage. This is quite important to her actually, as canaries don't have black and white vision at all, although their eyes do have fantastic colour vision.

What this means, is, they can't see at all well in dim light. This in turn means that a hen will always choose a fairly bright spot to build her nest, for she knows that it will be essential to be able to see her nestlings clearly in order to be able to feed them.

Once she has decided where to build her nest, things move fast; in less than 4 hours this hen's nest goes from bare liner to fully completed nest.

Make sure that you leave enough clearance above the nest when you hang it— by the time the chicks are almost ready to leave the nest, the parents will need all of a good six inches or so, in order to be able to feed their babies.

No matter what kind of nest you choose, you will need a liner for it. Most sources for breeding supplies also sell felt liners cut to fit the average-sized nestpan; these were traditionally sewn onto the nest to anchor them. Many people these days like to use double-sided carpet tape to anchor their nest liners. I myself usually use children's glue; I've found it works well enough for the month or two it is needed, comes free with a good tug, and washes out well once it is time to clean out the nest and liner.

You can, if you like, buy your own felt, and cut your own liners— just use one of the store-bought liners for a pattern, and be careful not to buy chemically treated felt. Remember though, that felt liners are not reusable and should be thrown away after one use.

Some people don't bother with the extra insulation offered by a liner, and just use a paper liner. The small basket-style coffee filter papers work well, these can be taped or glued to the nest, and will act as an adequate base to anchor the nesting material, although without offering the extra insulation and padding a felt liner offers.

Without some kind of liner between the nesting material and the smooth nestpan, the hen will not be able to build a nest secure enough to support the eggs and chicks adequately— the materials will slip and roll about in the nest when she climbs in or out, and the eggs will be likely to be damaged before hatching, if they don't just get tumbled right out, that is. Even worse, should she manage to incubate them to hatching, the chicks could too easily be accidentally pushed out of the nest.

I like to use washable crocheted nest liners. I first won a batch in a bird-raffle, and was instantly converted once I had tried them. I find them very useful, since they are easily washed, and can be re-used time after time. They make a perfect base for an excellent nest, particularly if you are using the burlap nest material recommended in Chapter 20.

Scale — 1 inch equals 4 double crochet stitches. The liner should measure from approx 2 to 2 inches from the edge of the inner circle to the outside edge of the liner. Use Crochet Hook E or #4.

- 1st row: Chain 8 - Join with slip stitch - forms a circle
- 2nd row: Chain 2, 16 dc (double crochet) stitches in joined circle and turn
- 3rd row: Chain 2, 1 dc in first stitch, 2 dc in next 12 stitches, 1 dc ea in last 2 stitches - turn
- 4th row: Chain 2, 1 dc in first stitch, 2 dc in next 24 stitches, 1 dc ea in last 2 stitches - turn
- 5th row: Chain 2, 1 dc stitch in each of nest 51 stitches - turn
- 6th row: Chain 1, 1 sc (single crochet) stitch in each dc stitch, turn *(The 6th row is optional, & can be used if you need to make the liner a tad bigger. I've used this in some liners, but have not needed it in others. May depend on the yarn you are using.)*
- 7th row: Chain 2, 1 dc stitch, skip next stitch, dc in next 46 stitches, skip one dc, dc in next 2 stitches
- 8th row: Chain 1, single crochet around the entire perimeter of the nest liner, tie off and weave the end in.

Chapter 14
The Incredible Egg

by Jim Clever

A bird's egg is nature's way of reproducing the species and contains all the essential nutrients for life. All the required nutrients are packed into the yolk and *albumen* (egg white) before it is laid, since the egg is a sealed unit. A fertile egg must contain the exact amount of water, protein, carbohydrates, minerals, vitamins and fats that are needed, since any deficiency will reduce the embryo's ability to grow, hatch and survive.

The female *gamete*, the ovum, is the largest cell known to science; but the male cell (*gamete*), the spermatozoon, is truly microscopic. However, the nucleus of the ovum is a tiny white 'speck', smaller than a pinhead, found on top of the egg-yolk; this is where the sperm (the male gamete) must 'drill' into the ovum and combine its DNA with that of the female gamete to form the new living embryo.

One of the author's canaries
(photo by Michael de Freitas)

The delicate structures of the egg are 'assembled' in four precise stages:

1. First the yolk and ovum develop in the ovary, among a 'grape-like' cluster of similar ovules, or miniature yolks. The yolk, together with its unfertilized *blastoderm*, (the ovum), matures in the ovary until it is released into the *infundibulum* (the upper funnel) of the oviduct, where it encounters the male sperm and is fertilized.

2. The fertilized egg with its microscopic embryo now passes down to the *magnum* (the upper middle section of the oviduct), where a layer of watery *albumen* (the egg-white) envelops the yolk in a thin sack. At opposite ends of the yolk, thin strands of albumen become twisted to form the rope-like *chalaza*; these two cords suspend the yolk centrally in a floating 'hammock' as it travels down the oviduct— the chalaza prevents the yolk from rising to bruise itself against the shell membranes. Before the yolk leaves the magnum the remaining volume of watery albumen is wrapped around it.

3. The developing egg then enters the *isthmus* (the lower mid-section of the oviduct), where the yolk and albumen are completely encapsulated in two loose-fitting shell membranes.

4. The egg then passes on to the *uterus*, where the final stage of egg formation occurs. About 80% of the egg's development is spent in the uterus; here the shell membranes tighten around the yolk and albumen, and the outer eggshell is finally secreted.

Once the shell has hardened, the finished egg passes down to the *cloaca* and is laid. This whole process takes about 24 hours.

The hen lays one egg per day, until she has a clutch of 3 to 6 eggs, depending on the breed of canary. She then incubates them for 13 days, and our 'small treasures' hatch into the next generation of 'show winners'!

Inside the Incredible Egg

The development of the canary embryo is a progressive, systematic, step-by-step process. There is a definite timetable for the development of each part of the chick's body. Keep those canary hens content and quiet with minimal disturbance, supply them with adequate food and water, and they will reward you with a clutch of tiny, bobbing heads, gaping mouths, and your next generation of potential 'show winners'.

Temperature is the most critical factor for the development of the embryo inside a canary egg. If the temperature rises above or falls below the optimum incubation range, life ends. Believe it or not, this optimum temperature falls within a very narrowly defined range of just half a degree, from 99.5°F–100°F (37.5°C - 37.78°C) for *all* species of birds. The body temperature of an incubating chicken is 107°F, while that of a setting canary hen may reach 110°F, but the temperature inside the eggs of both species must never exceed 100°F.

The hen achieves this by constantly turning and rearranging her clutch. The surface of the egg may be warmer when in direct contact with the hen's 'brood patch', but she carefully turns and rotates her eggs so that the interior of the egg remains a nearly constant 100°F.

The germinal disc, the *blastoderm*, of a fertilized egg, begins to develop even before the egg leaves the warm confines of the hen's body. Within two hours of fertilization, the newly formed cell, containing half the DNA of each parent, divides to form two cells.

Cell division continues so that by the time the egg is laid, a ball of undifferentiated cells sits on the upper surface of the egg yolk, where it will soon become the embryo. When the egg is laid in the nest, the internal temperature falls below 80°F (26.7°C), cell-division stops and the egg becomes dormant. (This is why it is so important, if you 'pull' eggs, that you store them in a cool area between 50–65°F.)

Eggs stored at 80°F or above will cause a slow growth of these cells that results in the eventual weakening and death of the embryonic cells. Storing eggs at temperatures below 40°F (4.4°C) will also kill these fertile cells.

Once the canary hen begins incubating her eggs, and they reach the correct internal temperature, a number of events occur in rapid succession. This sequence is remarkable!

On the First Day:
    10th hour - minute canary embryo is visible

> **11th hour** - alimentary (digestive) tract forms
> **12th hour** - vertebral column starts to develop
> **13th hour** - head begins to form
> **15th hour** - heart and eyes begin to form
> **21st hour** - ear formation begins

Second Day – The heart begins beating, legs and wings begin to grow, and the tongue and nostrils start to form.

Third Day – The formation of reproductive organs and differentiation of gender occurs.

Fourth Day – The beak begins to form

Fifth Day – Down and feather follicles begin to form

Sixth Day – The beak begins to harden

Seventh Day – The halfway point! All the above-mentioned tissues and organs continue to develop.

Eighth Day – The appearance of leg scales and toenails.

Ninth Day – A critical event occurs; the embryo changes position so that its head and shoulders are at the 'blunt' end of the egg.

Tenth Day - Scales, toenails, and beak firm and harden. The beak turns toward the air chamber.

Eleventh Day – The yolk sac starts to be absorbed into the body cavity.

Twelfth Day – The canary chick fills all the space in the egg except the air chamber.

Thirteenth Day - Neck spasms triggered by rising carbon dioxide levels within the egg, cause the chick to break into the air chamber and take its first breath.
Carbon dioxide levels begin to rise again as the chick consumes the oxygen in the air chamber.

Abdominal contractions suck the yolk sac into the chick's body. Neck, abdominal, and back-muscle spasms occur causing the chick to *pip* a hole in the egg— and the hatching process begins.

Fourteenth Day – A new canary chick.

The Miracle of the Hatching Egg

As the embryo of the fertile canary egg develops, the chick gradually transfers its head from the egg's pointed end, toward the air chamber in the blunt end, and tucks its head under its right wing. Since the unhatched egg is a closed system, there is little exchange of gases between the embryo and the external environment.

As the chick grows, blood, gases and nutrients circulate in the *allantoid*, a membranous sac that develops from the posterior part of the alimentary canal in the embryos of mammals, birds, and reptiles. But as the chick grows, the exchange of gases within the allantoid eventually fails to meet the needs of the developing chick.

A newly hatched canary chick.

The rising level of carbon dioxide within the egg eventually triggers spasms in the neck muscles of the embryo, causing the chick's head to jerk until its beak ruptures the membrane of the air chamber at the broad end of the egg.

The chick takes its first breath and its lungs begin to function as it breathes the air within this chamber. At this time the left-right cardio-vascular shunt in the embryo's immature heart closes and the heart-lung system begins to function normally. The elevated carbon dioxide levels also cause the abdominal muscles to contract, pulling the external yolk sac within the abdominal cavity, where it is slowly absorbed.

As the chick consumes the oxygen in the air chamber, the carbon dioxide level rises again to as much as 10%, triggering contractions in the neck muscles. During one of these spasms, the *egg tooth* on the chick's beak chips through the eggshell, forming a *pip* hole, which allows fresh oxygen to enter the air chamber.

Now, the chick begins to struggle for its life. Muscle spasms of the neck, back, and abdomen force the chick to wriggle and rotate its position from the first pip hole, ever so slightly. The neck muscle contracts again and another chip is made alongside the first. These small perforations, or *pips*, are always made in a counter-clockwise direction.

The chick rotates its position, a muscle spasm occurs, another chip in the shell is made, and so on, until a ring of perforations girdles the shell. Eventually, the chick has chipped away enough of the shell to loosen this 'cap' and it begins to kick with its legs, levering away the cap to escape from its prison.

In a small species like the canary, the entire process from breaking into the air chamber and pipping the shell takes about three hours. The interval from pipping to kicking free from the egg can take as little as 30 minutes, if conditions are right.

A number of fatal flaws can occur during the final hours of development and hatching; three that result in *dead-in-shell* chicks are described here.

1. It often happens, if an egg is more rounded than oval in shape, that the chick ends up with its head at the wrong end of the egg, away from the air chamber. This is lethal in most cases because the chick cannot penetrate the air chamber to obtain its first breath, and suffocates.

2. Similarly, if the chick's head becomes trapped under

its left wing, rather than its right wing, this will be fatal in nearly all cases. The chick is genetically 'programmed' to turn counter-clockwise as it pips the shell, but if the head is locked beneath the left wing, its body gets in the way and pipping cannot take place.

3. Finally, if the chick's feet are positioned above its head, this will also be lethal, since it will be unable to kick free of the shell.

So once again nature gives us the 'little gift' of a newly hatched canary. But the true miracle really is that this frail little bundle of life is able to hatch at all!

* References:

1). Olsen GH, Duval F: Commonly Encountered Hatching Problems, 'Proceedings of the Association of Avian Veterinarians, 1994, pp379-385.

2). Richie BW, Harrison GL, Harrison LR, editors: Avian Medicine: Principles and Applications, Lake Worth, FL, 1994, pp457-478.

3). Stromberg, J., A Guide to Better Hatching, Stromberg Publishing Co., Fort Dodge, IA 1975 Cornell Extension Bulletin 205, Cornell University, Ithaca, NY

Chapter 15
Laying Eggs & Raising Chicks

Rather than discussing the ins and outs of the stages of nesting, hatching, and raising the chicks, I thought it might be more illustrative of the process to show you the highlights of a month in the life of a pair of breeding canaries, as caught by the Canary Cam in the spring of 2000.

6:34:53 AM:

Dawn breaks on a new day— and it is time for this canary hen, who I call 'Dolly', to lay the last egg of her clutch.

Most canary hens lay their eggs early in the dawn, before the bird-room lights come on, but as summer creeps closer, the day comes when there is enough light for the Cam to be able to document this fascinating natural process.

Each egg masses approximately 25% of the hen's total body weight. To put this into perspective, this is equivalent to a human woman weighing 100 pounds giving birth to a 25-pound baby!

6:52:55 AM:
 The light is growing swiftly now, and she stands in her nest and begins to strain. The egg is huge in relation to the size of her body, and she must pass it or die trying.

6:53:59 AM:

The difficulty of her chore shows in the stiffness of her stance and the gaping beak—laying an egg is perhaps the most demanding task she will ever perform in her lifetime.

6:56:38 AM:
 She cannot stop or rest until the egg is passed. Restless, she moves about in the nest. She shifts her stance and strains mightily yet again...

6:59:47 AM:
 The egg has crested and drops into the nest, and Dolly begins to relax. Her egg laid, she allows herself a brief rest while it dries, giving herself a chance to catch her breath. Then, her early morning ordeal behind her, it's off to get some breakfast!

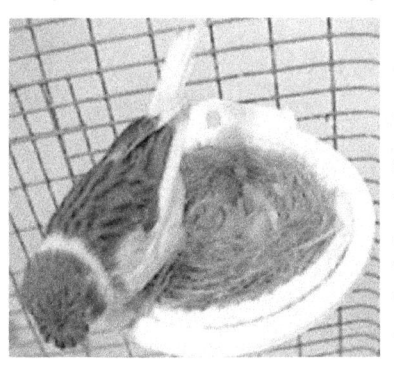

7:07:39 AM: 
The sun is fully up now. Her morning chore over, Dolly settles to her job. She will incubate and turn the eggs until they are due to hatch, in 13 days or so. The days pass, and hatching draws near. Since she was set with one egg a day earlier than the other three, one chick should hatch a day earlier than the rest. This way Dolly can practice feeding for a day before the rest of the chicks hatch, rather than being required to tackle four hungry chicks all at once. Finally the first chick begins to hatch. Slowly it chips its way around the inside of the eggshell, until a definite gap shows. Quietly she calls to Dan to alert him. He drops everything and hussles over to the nest to greet his new hatchling. Heads together, his parents hover closely over the chick, encouraging its efforts to hatch.

It must be allowed room to get out of the shell, but it could suffer from heat-loss if allowed too much space too fast. Instinctively they know to give him just enough room and no more. They also know that at this stage all they can do is to encourage the chick verbally, which they do using tiny, sweet-voiced calls.

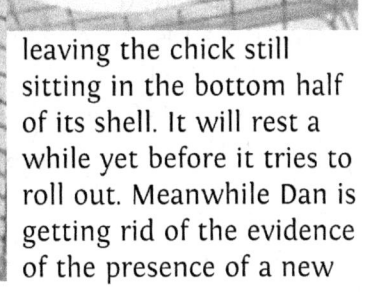

Dan goes off to eat, and when he returns, Dolly leaves him on guard while she eats in turn. Dan watches closely as his chick slowly pushes the top of his shell the last little way off. A few seconds later the top half flips free, and he reaches in and gently removes the empty piece of shell, leaving the chick still sitting in the bottom half of its shell. It will rest a while yet before it tries to roll out. Meanwhile Dan is getting rid of the evidence of the presence of a new hatchling by taking the eggshell as far as possible from the nest and hiding it. When he returns, Dolly is sitting on the nest. He tries to reach under her to feed the chick, and she gives him a warning glare— he is *not* to feed the chick without her okay!

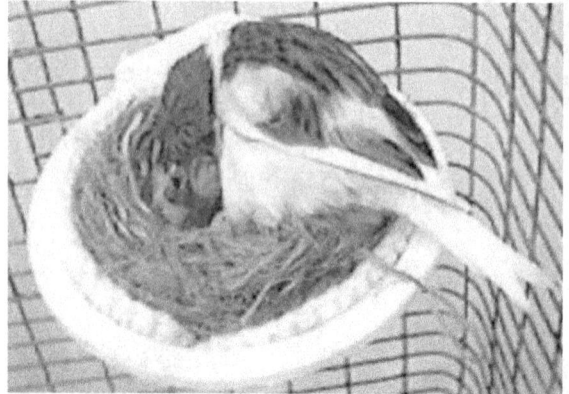

Seeming rather abashed, he beats a hasty retreat, leaving mother and new chick to share a peaceful moment over the chick's first meal a few hours later, once the egg sac is entirely absorbed. Slowly, tenderly, a tiny bit at a time, she feeds him. Early the next morning, Dan is in for a big surprise— the rest of the chicks are hatching! He got over his surprise in a hurry when he found that Dolly was going to let him help feed though! Both parents hop to work, busily stuffing any open mouth they can see, and it's not long before all four little heads are hungrily reaching up for more food...and more food. The chicks will continue their rapid growth, and when Dolly isn't supervising Dan, she is demanding that he hurry up and bring more food to fill their almost endless appetites. Willingly, he obliges her, feeding his rapidly growing brood while his mate alternates with him. Until their chicks are fledged and fully weaned, this will be their daily routine, without varying. Their only goal is to feed their young. They will stop every once in a while to eat and clean the nest of

Brats in Feathers; Keeping Canaries

any fecal matter or other foreign substance, and every once in a while they will even feed each other— when they're not feeding babies, that is.

As you can see in the top right photo, getting the babies fed can include getting into some rather strange positions! But Dolly & Dan don't seem to care, as long as the job still gets done.

On average, a canary chick grows so fast it literally doubles its weight daily for the first 10 days or so. This allows it to reach a size close to that of an adult in the space of two short weeks. This is a species survival trait, since it gives a wild chick the best chance of survival. It's a trait still shared by most songbirds, including canaries, to this day.

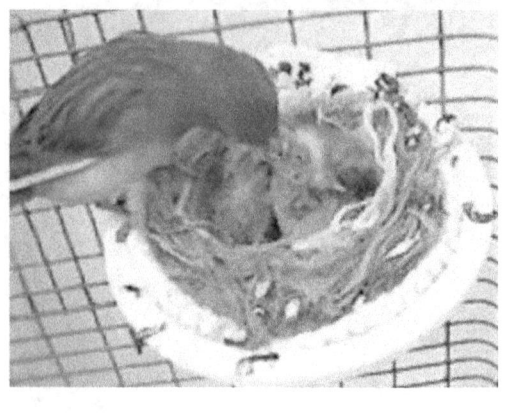

Around the time the chick's legs get strong enough to allow them to reach the edge of the nest, they will start to deposit their droppings over the edge, rather than in the bottom of the nest. At about the same time Dolly & Dan stop cleaning the inside of the nest, no longer removing the droppings. By the time the chicks are ready to fledge, the outer edge of the nest will have quite a crust built up around the edge, but the inside of the nest should still be fairly clean.

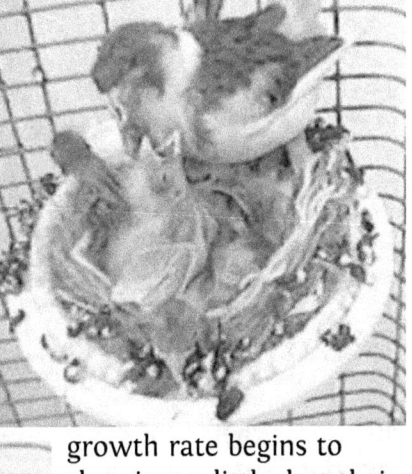

If this is not the case, it means the nest is too deep; in such cases it's quite easy to just add a handful of nest material to the bottom of the nest when banding the chicks.

As the pin feathers begin to show, the chicks' growth rate begins to slow just a little, but their demand for food increases. Growing in feathers takes a lot of energy! Both parents work ceaselessly to keep their brood fed, with no sign of growing tired of their endless chore. I have often wondered if those little mouths seem as bottomless to them as they do to me!

As their feathers develop, the chicks begin to be a little more aware of their surroundings, and spend less time sleeping or eating, and more time stretching or just gazing around at the scenery, learning about the world.

The picture on the left shows one chick aiming over the edge of the nest, while his mother feeds two of his siblings. Meanwhile Dan is down at the food dish filling up his crop, only to empty it into those hungry, waiting, open mouths.

Occasionally both parents arrive at the nest together, but more often they space their feedings to arrive separately The chicks are now 10 days old, and their body feathers are filling in nicely. Every day shows visible changes, when you grow as fast as a healthy canary chick! I sometimes think it is a wonder their parents manage to keep them fully fed, they eat so much and digest so fast.

If you look closely at the next two photos, you will see the birdie bath tub hanging just to the left side of the nest; this is the kind I prefer to use. I always make sure that the water is shallower than usual when the chicks are this age, to help prevent the possibility of an accident; I don't need anybody taking any unexpected dunkings. The chicks' feathers are almost completely grown in now, with the exception of the tail feathers and some of the final wing feathers. The last body feathers will unfurl around the head and face, making things a little easier to keep clean in case their parents miss now and then, while feeding— at this age, those little heads bob around a lot!

By fourteen days old, the chicks are almost adult size, and their feathers are close to being fully unfurled, even those on their faces. They are beginning to spend a a lot of their time preening their new feathers, allowing the Cam to catch the shot below, showing three chicks in an identical pose, while the fourth, almost completely hidden, rests in the middle of the nest. But as adult as they are growing to be, they are still quite young and still *very* interested in eating when Mom or Dad should happen to show up with lunch!

When they are not eating or preening, the chicks practice flying, while holding firmly onto the nest with their feet. They are now seventeen and sixteen days old, and are so large that only one can fit into the nest, forcing each in turn to spend some time gathered on the nest edge with the rest, watching everything going on in their vicinity.

In the morning of his 18th day, the eldest chick looks over the edge of the nest and sees his mother and father eating their breakfast on the cage floor below. His nestmates don't notice when he decides to join his parents, and leaps over the edge of the nest. He will be back again & again over the next few days, as he gradually learns how to fend for himself; but he won't linger long, and never again will he return to stay.

Chapter 16
Record-Keeping

Keeping proper records is very important if you intend to continue breeding for more than a year or two. Your records will be the basis for all your future pairings, and will give you the ability to trace your birds' lineage when you need to— and while you may not realize it at the beginning, sooner or later you *will* need to refer to something other than your memory.

Properly kept records will also come in handy when it comes time to sell any birds you have bred but won't be keeping. Although you may think, at first at least, that you will just keep any youngsters you breed, a year or two of successful breeding will show you that this is just not possible.

It is usually fairly easy to sell excess youngsters to a wholesaler, but I don't recommend this— selling to these dealers only supports and encourages the continuance of 'pet mill' trade— only too active in the bird world. Selling directly to the people who will be keeping your birds is quite a lot more work, but this way you can be assured that the people who are buying them know the basics of caring for their new bird properly, and will appreciate the work you put into raising them.

Either way, being able to keep a record of who bought which bird, can not only come in handy, but on occasion can literally turn out to be a life-saver— for the bird, at least.

Especially when are selling to another breeder, being able to include a chart showing the ancestry of the bird being sold gives a positive impression of your professionalism, and adds assurance that they have made a good choice in buying their new stock from you.

There are many ways to keep your records— almost every canary breeder you will meet with more than a year or two's worth of breeding canaries under his or her belt will almost certainly have their own preferred method.

Many breeders rely on computer programs to keep track of their records. There are many different kinds of these programs available, depending on your needs and what you wish to pay. Of these, some prefer the programs developed for keeping livestock records, while others swear by the ones developed for keeping track of human families.

Most of these programs are adaptable, and it is often fairly easy to adapt the field names and data to your own needs & preference. Many even come with a free trial, so if you like you can try several, and see which one works best for you.

One of Robirda's young red canaries, looking quite calm about his photo-session.   (*photo by Michael de Freitas*)

No matter what method you end up using, it's a good idea to make sure you will be able to record as much detail as possible, one way or another. The time will eventually come when having this information available to you will prove to be not only invaluable, but necessary to your continuing success.

If you are like me and prefer to be able to see and hold your information, rather than viewing it on a screen, then you may choose to keep your records on paper rather than electronically. This method is a little more work, perhaps, but I find it is also much more adaptable and, for me at least, more satisfying.

Whichever method you choose, electronic or paper, the same basic rules should apply– choose your method to suit your needs, and feel free to adapt it as necessary until you are comfortable with the results. Make certain you will be able to include and easily access all the detail you need, whenever you should happen to need it.

My own method uses a loose-leaf booklet, with one page per breeding pair, and tabs to separate each year's group. Each breeding cage is numbered, and each sheet is headed up by the year, the cage number, and the *family band* (if I need it, I don't always).

What is a family band? It's an option I sometimes include, and sometimes don't; the definition can vary from breeder to breeder. For me, it is a coloured plastic band that I put on all chicks who hatch in the same nest. This gives me a visual aid to help ensure that I don't accidentally inbreed.

What this all means is that my records pages appear rather like the example on the following page.

You will note that I've allowed room for only two nests per pair. This is deliberate; yes, sometimes it is possible to get more, but in the long run doing so is counter-productive, and will compromise the health of the adult canaries. The stress caused by the great effort required won't show until breeding season ends and the moult begins, but when it does begin to show, it will be unmistakeable. Too many canaries don't survive their moult, after such stress.

While the following page may seem to include a lot of data, I find it provides me with the information I need in order to know how closely I have managed to come in any current year to my goals.

Robirda McDonald

Year_____ Cage #_____ Family Band_____

Cock_____ Band #_____

Hen_____ Band #_____

Cock's Parents_____ Family Band_____

Hen's Parents_____ Family Band_____

NEST # 1

Date 1st egg_____   Total eggs_____

Date Set_____   Date Due_____

Candled_____   # Fertile_____

Date Hatched_____   Total chicks___

Description of Young   Band #

_____   _____
_____   _____
_____   _____
_____   _____
_____   _____

NEST # 2

Date 1st egg_____   Total eggs_____

Date Set_____   Date Due_____

Candled_____   # Fertile_____

Date Hatched_____   Total chicks___

Description of Young   Band #

_____   _____
_____   _____
_____   _____
_____   _____
_____   _____

Breeding Notes_____
_____

Show Notes_____
_____

BIRDS SOLD:

Name_____   Name_____

Phone_____Band#_____   Phone_____Band#_____

Name_____   Name_____

Phone_____Band#_____   Phone_____Band#_____

Name_____.   Name_____

Phone_____Band#_____   Phone_____Band#_____

When planning pairs for an upcoming breeding season, I often make up lineage or pedigree charts for planning matings, to accompany my current breeding records page. I find that comparing charts gives me a better grasp of the characteristics and genetic heritage of each bird than looking at any number of breeding record pages. But in the end, it's what works for you that counts, so don't be afraid to try different methods to find out what will work best.

A pedigree can span as many generations as you have records for, and puts all the information for each individual on one page. At a glance, you can see the entire history of each bird's family.

I usually lay out my charts something like the following example. You can go back as many generations as you like (or have room for). For each entry on the chart record the band number, a brief description, the year bred, and the breeder's name.

Father	Paternal Grandfather	Great-Grandfather
		Great-Grandmother
	Paternal Grandmother	Great-Grandfather
		Great-Grandmother
Mother	Maternal Grandfather	Great-Grandfather
		Great-Grandmother
	Maternal Grandmother	Great-Grandfather
		Great-Grandmother

This picture shows how to safely hold your canary. It is very important to be sure your fingers are under his jaw as shown, and be sure that you are putting *no* pressure on his ribs.

Chapter 17
Handling Canaries

Many canary owners, in particular new ones, are afraid to handle their bird. After all, they are very small, quite delicate, and quite obviously don't like being held in the slightest! They generally try as hard as possible to avoid being caught, and can get very stressed over the whole situation.

It's understandable enough, if you think about it. Canaries aren't very social, and don't engage in mutual preening, as do many other bird species. Their feathers are susceptible to damage from handling, and every instinct tells them that if they are caught, they will become somebody's dinner. But if you are going to be keeping one or more canaries, whether you like it or not, there will be times when catching and handling them will be just plain necessary.

The pictures at the head of the chapter at below show how to safely hold a canary in order to clip toenails, check for condition or signs of illness, administer medication, or any number of other reasons. It is very important to hold a canary correctly, because any pressure on the ribs can cause him to have trouble breathing, or even to suffocate— his ribs 'float', that is, they are anchored to the spine with cartilage, not bone, and his ability to breathe depends on his ribs being able to expand freely.

A safe hold is quite easy, and is accomplished by simply putting your index and middle finger around his neck just under the jaw, and curling the rest of your hand lightly around his body, with the wings tucked into the palm of your hand.

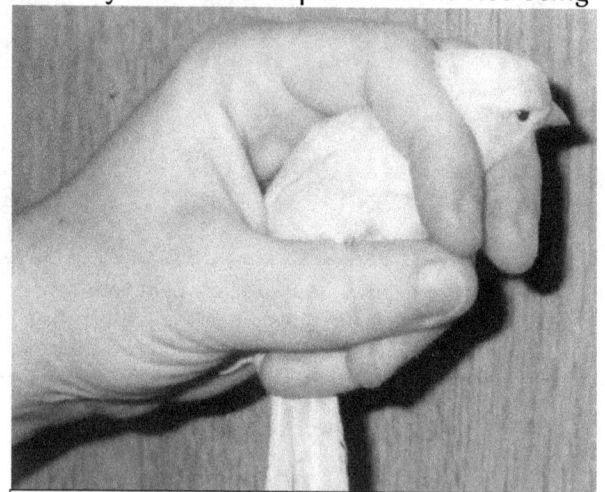

Here is the same hold, shown at a different angle. Note how the bird can easily grip the thumb with his feet; this helps him to remain calmer.

These pictures each show the same method for grasping a canary safely, but from a slightly different angle. Can you see where he is grasping my thumb with his foot in the second picture? It helps to encourage them to do this, as it makes them feel more secure.

As you may be able to tell, he is not thrilled about being handled, particularly in the last shot where he is having his toenails trimmed, but he is not upset enough about it to be struggling, either. In fact, the item of most interest in his mind at the time these photos were taken lay in keeping an eye on that thing Mom kept fooling with!

The main restraint to this hold is the fingers under the jaw— make sure you have his *neck* between your fingers, and not his *head* or he might be able to wriggle free! Your fingers should be on either side of his neck just under and below his jawbone.

This photo shows the detail of cutting a canary's nails. As long as they are fine-tipped enough to be accurate, you can use any size of scissors or clippers— I like these larger ones because the extra-fine tip allows for better accuracy, while the size makes for easy handling. Nail clippers are okay too, but in my opinion don't offer a clear view of exactly where you are clipping, which is quite important.

Clipping nails. You can use nail-clippers or scissors, whatever you like, as long as you can see clearly exactly where you are cutting.

You need to work in a strong light, so that you can make sure that you can see where the end of the quick inside the nail is before you cut— if you snip this, you will have to deal with bleeding. Before you start, prepare for this accidental occurrence by placing a small cup of plain white flour within easy reach of where you will be working.

Never remove more than 1/3rd of a nail at one time, or you risk cutting into the quick. Should you accidentally cut too far down the nail, you can use a pinch of flour and a little pressure to stop the bleeding and encourage fast clotting. Overcut toenails rarely bleed heavily, but canaries don't have a lot of blood to spare, either.

I prefer plain white flour over something like a styptic pencil, because the styptic stings like fury, causing them to struggle. This upsets the birds needlessly, to my mind. Cornstarch works too, but doesn't encourage clotting as well as flour. You do want to be careful not to do what one person I know did, and accidentally grab the baking powder instead of the cornstarch! Baking powder will not only *not* stop bleeding, it can be dangerous for your bird.

Most canaries are quite calm throughout the nail-clipping process, if held correctly. They can breathe easily, and are able to grasp one of your fingers with one foot, while you are working on the other. Try not to be nervous, as it will affect the bird you are holding— just proceed slowly, being careful not to clip anything but toenails, one toe at a time— and before you know it, you will be done.

Especially if you are going to breed canaries, it's a good idea to make a point of handling your birds on a regular basis. Besides keeping on top of the usual maintenance issues such as keeping toenails clipped, it helps to establish a routine where you regularly check each bird over and note general health issues such as the condition of their vents, the amount of padding present (or not) around the keel bone, the density and proper growth of feathers, etc.

Skimpy feathering can indicate a lack of minerals, in particular calcium or iodine— or an overly low supply of the vitamins necessary to metabolize needed minerals— or both.

This kind of routine not only helps you to keep an eye on your bird's health and general state of being, but also, and perhaps more importantly, allows the birds to get used to being handled by you, and to learn that nothing harmful will happen to them while being handled by you. In fact, if you make sure to offer them a favoured treat every time you're done, it may not be long before you find them looking forward to the experience, perhaps even allowing themselves to be caught easily and without any protest!

Being used to being handled by you will also tend to make them a little calmer when they have new babies in the nest and you need to do your regular maintenance routines in their cage– and it makes such chores as close-banding easier, too, simply by reducing the hen's tendency to be suspicious of you. A win-win situation if ever there was one!

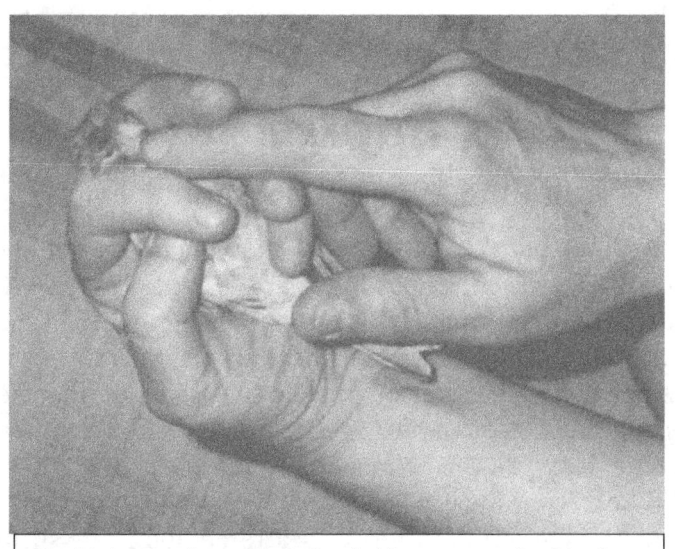

If a bird struggles while being held, you can calm him by stroking him gently on the throat beginning directly below the beak, as shown in this photo.

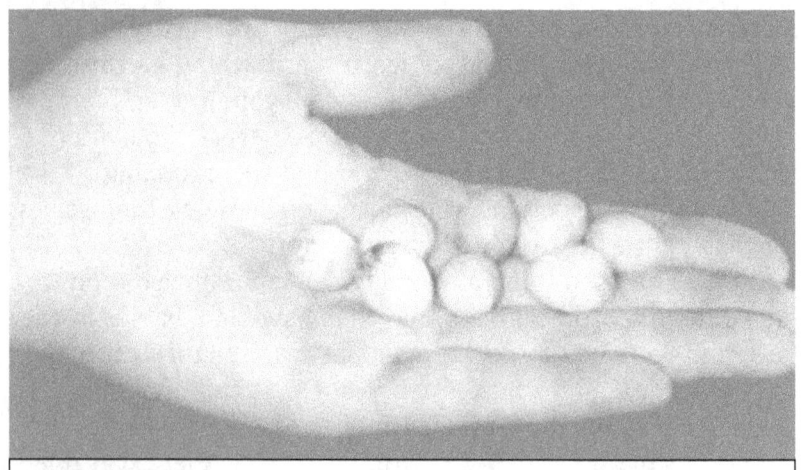

A handful of canary eggs. The colour normally ranges from pale to darkish blue or blue-green, sometimes with some brown or black speckling. Yes, each canary chick hatches out of an egg this size!

Chapter 18
Handling & Candling Canary Eggs

The handful of canary eggs shown above, each one from a different hen, shows how canary eggs can vary. The colour can range from almost white through the light blues to a darker, almost muddy greenish-blue. Size will vary too— some hens will lay larger or smaller eggs than another hen of the same size. Most canary eggs, though, will be a rather pale blue, very like the colour of a robin's egg.

Sometimes you will see speckles of a lighter red-brown, or a darker black-brown scattered about the surface of the eggshell. While these markings do often tend to cluster on the bigger end of the egg, they can occur anywhere, and indicate that the chick within will have the ability to display melanin— if there is any melanin in the feathers, that is. I have found that chicks from more heavily marked eggs will very often show quite a lot of melanin.

Proper handling of the eggs is very important.

Eggshells are not as solid as we tend to think they are. They are actually a little porous; they need to be for the chick inside to be able to develop properly.

This porosity means that water, oil, bacteria, and other such substances can affect the eggs and change their chances for a successful hatching. This in turn means that whenever you are going to be handling eggs, it is *extremely* important to wash your hands thoroughly beforehand.

Drying your hands well is important too. When a hen lays an egg, her body adds a light coating over the surface of the egg. This coating helps the shell to stay as resistant as possible to foreign bacteria. It is, however, water soluble, which means that wet hands could remove part of this protective coating. Better if your hands are not only be clean, but good and dry when you handle your canaries' eggs.

You may say that you don't plan to ever handle the eggs at all. I know people who successfully do this, too. They use such tools as melon-ball scoops to pick up and put down each egg that they must move.

This is fine, if that is what you prefer— but having tried both methods, I find it both simpler and safer to handle the eggs myself, and to know how to do it safely. What if my hands shake and the egg rolls around in the spoon and addles itself? ('Addling' means, scrambled inside the shell. Needless to say, an addled egg will not hatch.)

In my experience it is a rare breeder who does not have to handle his or her birds' eggs— at least occasionally. And when you do, I believe it's a good idea to know how to do it properly. After all, you want successful hatchings, not chicks dead in their shells from improper egg handling or storage!

The picture on the next page illustrates how to correctly hold any egg, even one so small and delicate as the canary egg. When held end-to-end, or, 'pole-to-pole', as some people put it, all eggs are quite strong, and you will have to apply deliberate pressure in order to break it.

If the egg does break when being handled this way, it means that the hen who laid it was lacking in adequate minerals to allow her body to form a proper eggshell— perhaps she does not have adequate minerals available, OR she may be lacking in the vitamins necessary to digest them. If you do find such an egg, you will know that the hen who laid it narrowly avoided being eggbound, and that her diet requires immediate attention; supplementation of more calcium and trace minerals, along with the vitamins needed to digest them (in particular D, C, and B), must be provided ASAP.

Even a strong egg is actually quite delicate, handled incorrectly— if you should try to pick a canary egg up from any other angle, you will find that out just how frail that pretty little pale blue shell really is!

Sett your hen, as the old term for allowing a hen to start incubating is, once the final egg in the clutch is laid. Usually this is fairly obvious, because with most canary hens, the final egg will be a deeper, richer blue than the rest of the clutch. If you happen to have one of the rare hens who doesn't lay a 'blue' final egg, simply wait until you are not finding an egg every morning before setting her with the clutch.

Many breeders will tell you they sett their hens with their eggs at four or five days after the first egg was laid; this

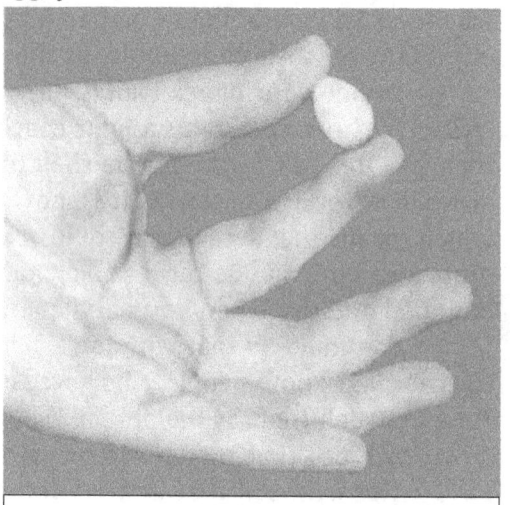

How to correctly hold a tiny canary egg easily, safely & securely.

is fine if a hen only lays four or five eggs, but if she should happen to lay another egg the day after the rest of the clutch is sett, one of the babies will hatch a day later. This means it will have a much slimmer chance of survival. Ill or dead nestmates can cause problems for the entire clutch, so it's much safer to prevent any such problem if you can, by making sure there will be no more eggs laid before allowing the hen to begin incubating.

Candling is a process used to discern whether the eggs a breeding hen is incubating are fertile. The proper term *is* 'sett', by the way— a resting hen sits on her perch, but an incubating hen *setts* her eggs.

The term *candling* is also quite old, and refers to the method originally used to test eggs for fertility. A lit taper candle was placed into a closed tin holder that had a small hole punched into the side. This allowed a small amount of light to shine through. Each egg was carefully picked up and held so that it blocked the light coming from the tin, forcing it to shine through the egg.

When looked at in this way, the eggshell becomes semi-translucent, and it is possible to see if there is an embryo developing within the egg. An infertile egg will simply show a blank yolk, while a developing chick will show as a dark mass.

The best time to candle an egg is approximately half ways through incubation, six or seven days into the process. By then the embryo will be well developed enough to be clearly present. Try not to candle a canary egg after 10 days or so of incubation, there's a chance you could cause some damage to the eyes. If you candle the egg too early, you will not be able to tell whether or not an embryo is forming. To a certain extent, the brighter the light you use to candle the egg with, the more clearly you will be able to see the developing chick.

You can buy special tools for candling eggs— one of the best is a small bright light on the end of a flexible extension, that allows you to easily direct the light behind every egg in a nest to check for fertility, and never have to touch an egg. If you are careful, a penlight with a bright halogen bulb can serve the same purpose for much less cost, or you can rig an affair rather like the old-timer's candling tool using a flashlight and a shoebox (or something similar).

If you feel you absolutely must remove infertile or unhatched eggs from the nest, you must replace them with fake eggs— or marbles, or anything else of a non-toxic, non-absorbent material of about the right size.

This is because the chicks, once hatched, require the support of either their nest mates or the other eggs from the clutch, in order to see that the soft bones of the feet and legs develop properly. Actually, it's not a bad idea to replace all unhatched eggs with fakes— this prevents accidental breakage that could produce a very smelly mess or even contaminate the nest.

On occasion you will see birds where the long bones of the leg bent out while the chick was growing; this is known as *splayed leg* and is due to one of two causes; either there was inadequate dietary supplies while in the nest of the vitamins and minerals needed by the fast-growing chick, or, more usually, the problem was caused by the chick having not had enough support from other eggs or other chicks in the nest while growing.

Take the necessary care to handle your birds' eggs properly, when you must, allowing them to fulfill their full evolutionary role, and you will reap a marvelous reward; fertile eggs that hatch into lovely young canaries to fill your home with song.

A handful of Robirda's soak seed mix at the best stage for feeding canaries with youngsters in the nest; this is when protein content is at it's highest.

Chapter 19
Soak Seed & Nestling Food

Soaked seed is a method of feeding seed in a form similar to that in which it is often found in the wild by a foraging bird. As the name implies, this method involves soaking the seed, followed by thorough rinsing and (usually) a short period in which the soaked seed is allowed to begin to sprout.

Wild birds eat many varieties of green and/or sprouting seeds in their quest for food. Seed in this form is highly nutritious.

Nestling food is what canary breeders call the dry mix on which they base the food they give to parent birds who are feeding babies. A number of items are often added to this dry mix just before serving, among them being water, eggs that have been boiled then chopped or grated, grated carrots, crushed baby biscuits...the different mixes and methods vary almost as much as do canary breeders.

A good nestling food, which the birds like and will readily feed to their chicks, is a necessary and nutritious addition to the breeding canary's diet. It needs to be able to fulfill the constant requirements of the rapidly growing canary youngster, so must be quite high in nutrient content.

This means nestling food is also a useful dietary supplement year round even for adults, but care must be taken not to feed too much outside of the breeding season; just as with people, overdoing rich foods can result in painful diseases such as gout, liver disease, or heart disease.

Commercially made nestling foods provide an easy and usually fairly reliable way to keep your canaries healthy and happy no matter what time of year it is. You will sometimes hear nestling food called "egg food". Don't be fooled, they're both basically the same thing.

I believe that soak seed and nestling food work best together, and how to do that is what this article is all about.

Starting Right With Soak Seed

You can use either your own soak seed mix or a commercial one. The seed must be fresh to sprout properly!

A basic make-your-own soak seed mix for canaries can consist of the following:
- 40% canary grass seed,
- 25% black oil sunflower seed,
- 10% canola seed, and
- 5% *each* of wheat berries, mung beans, safflower seed, raw sesame seed, and buckwheat.

Herman Bros and Silversong West have been making and marketing good soak seed mixes for some years now, and if you like, Herman Bros will even put together whatever kind of seed mix you want, especially for you. Both will ship your order to wherever you request if you can't buy their products locally, and both have websites where you can investigate their products.

Measure about 1 teaspoon dry soak seed mix per bird serving you wish to prepare. If you're feeding parent birds be sure to count each baby as one and a half birds— each chick needs a *lot* of food to support the rate at which it grows. Remember too, that they will need several servings a day while in the nest— otherwise one serving a day per bird will be plenty for most circumstances.

Place the dry seed in a jar or bowl and cover it with twice the amount of room temperature water. If you feel mould growth might be a problem (this will vary, depending on geographic location and time of year), add about a teaspoon of bleach per quart of water for prevention.

Some soaked seed sprouting in a sieve. Note the wad of wrung-out paper toweling underneath; this helps keep excess water from collecting in the bottom of the sieve.

Stir well, then let sit for about 12 hours or so. Then pour the seed into a nylon-mesh sieve, such as shown here, and rinse everything thoroughly under running water for several minutes.

Leave the seed in the sieve and immerse the entire affair in a fresh bowl of room temperature water so that the seed is covered, and leave it for another 6-10 hours or so. Remove from the water, rinse thoroughly as before, and now you may either serve it to the birds, or let it grow for another day or so.

If you wish to do the latter, a method that works well for me is to place the sieve in the dish drainer or an empty bowl. In order to discourage mold growth, a wad of wrung-out damp paper towel is placed underneath the sieve. This breaks the surface tension of the water in the sieve and prevents excessive water from collecting in the bottom of the sieve, which would encourage rot or mould. The sprouts must be rinsed thoroughly several times during the day. Squeeze excess water from the wad of paper toweling each time as well. After 24 hours or so of additional sprouting, you should refrigerate any sprouts you haven't yet served to the birds. They will usually keep for three or four days this way.

Serving Soak Seed & Nestling Food

While you can feed the soaked and slightly sprouted seeds alone, my favourite method of feeding them is to take about a tablespoon of sprouted seed per bird and add to the damp seed about a teaspoon of dry nestling food. Mix this thoroughly until you have a crumbly mixture, a little on the dry side rather than wet, and feed it to the birds. They find this mixture highly acceptable, and it raises beautiful baby birds, as well as keeping the adults in exceptional health and feather condition year round.

Use this mixture once or twice a week throughout the year as a conditioner and song stimulator, and for extra nutrition, feed it every day through the annual molt. For use as a breeding diet, serve this mixture fresh at *least* twice a day, but preferably three or four times a day when there are babies in the nest, and about two or three times a week for several weeks prior to hatching.

Remember, damp foods can go sour easily, and should remain in the cage only about an hour or so, a little longer if it is not too warm.

Increase the amount as the youngsters grow until at two weeks of age you are feeding about two tablespoons of mixture per bird per feeding. As they begin to learn to eat on their own, start to reduce the amount of nestling food in the mixture, substituting a little ground bread crumbs or some uncooked rolled oats if the mix gets too wet, until by six weeks of age or so there is next to no nestling food in the mix.

By now they should be eating fairly well on their own, and you can begin feeding them as adults. Include lots of soft foods such as greens daily until they are fully able to crack enough dry seed to support themselves, which can take until they are as much as twelve weeks of age.

Some commercial nestling foods contain fairly high quantities of sugar or honey— be very careful *not* to offer such a nestling food when the hatchlings are three days old, or younger— too much sugar is literally a poison for them, and can be a killer. If you are unable to find a good commercial nestling food you like, or have the time and would prefer to make your own, below you will find my recipe for homemade nestling food— I find this recipe works very well, and raises even healthier nestlings than most commercial mixes do!

At this point the seeds have sprouted enough to begin splitting the shells, allowing canaries to eat even such large seeds as black oil sunflower.

My recipe is based on dried 100% whole wheat bread. I get several loaves, tear them into bits, and oven-dry them at around 250 degrees (F) or so until they smell nutty and are bone dry. Then I whiz them, a few handfuls at a time, in a blender or a food processor until it's well ground. Then I mix 6 cups of these ground whole-wheat breadcrumbs with 2 cups of rolled oats, and 1 cup each of corn meal and cream of wheat (sometimes called *wheatlets*) – dry, not cooked.

To this mix is added around a half a cup of raw sesame seed, useful for both for its calcium content, and because it is high in lysine. Along with this I add a tablespoon of sea salt (preferably), or (alternatively) iodized table salt, and about double that of Hagen's 'Prime'.

You can also add a couple of tablespoons or so of canthaxanthin at this stage if you like, and want to colour-feed your canaries. Exactly how much you should offer per pound of mix will vary depending on which product you are using, so be sure to follow the instructions, which should be included. If you're in doubt, just monitor the droppings; any red colour showing means too much colouring is being given, you should cut back until the droppings look normal again.

I mix everything together thoroughly and store it in the freezer, or else as cool and dry a place as I can manage.

When I have moulting birds, weanlings, or birds that have been ill and are recuperating, they are given some of this mix daily, dusted on a good soak seed mix.

If I have youngsters in the nest, 2 cups of the breadcrumb mix is blended with 1 cup of the flaked instant baby-cereal (the kind without all the extra iron added) before being added to the soaked seed. Once the youngsters are fledged and out of the nest, I begin to reduce the amount of baby-cereal being added to the mix, reducing the total protein content of the mixture until by a week or two later I am adding none. At the same time I allow the sprouts to grow a little more, and begin to develop a little green.

These two actions change the mixture from the high-protein mixture the babies need when they are growing in the nest, to a vitamin-and-carbohydrate rich mixture that helps give the youngsters the energy they need while they learn to eat for themselves.

I find this an easy-to-use recipe that can be adapted easily depending on what it is needed for, from the high-protein diet needed for babies, to the requirements for higher starches and vitamins needed by moulting, weaning, or recuperating birds. It also makes a good stretcher for commercial egg foods, besides being cheap to make. And because there is no sugar in it, it is safe for even first-day hatchlings, unlike many commercial egg foods.

I find I get great results with this mixture, and I like the fact that it avoids all the mess of fixing eggs, as well as cutting all the extra fats (that are in the eggs) from the diet.

Because the combined nutrients from the soak seed mix blend with the ingredients in the nestling food mix to provide a balanced amount of protein, fats, vitamins and minerals, the birds still get adequate amounts of complete protein, including all the amino acids, when they are in the nest. (But do please note that all the ingredients listed in both the soak seed mix and the nestling food must be included in order to ensure a proper dietary balance). I hope you find this mix as useful as I do!

A Few Words of Caution

Remember when feeding any soft or wet food that you must remove it from the cage within a few hours, less if the temperature is hot. The warmer the weather, the faster soft foods can go sour— and if that happens, it can make your birds very sick, and maybe even kill them!

Please note that all moulds are very toxic to canaries; if you should happen to find any moulds forming on the seeds while they are soaking or sprouting, throw the whole lot out.

Never try to pick out the mouldy seeds; even if you think you removed it all you will have missed some. Always remember that you are dealing with foods that can be potentially harmful if sufficient attention is not paid.

This is a dominant white canary; it differs from the recessive white in that it has a little yellow visible on the butts of the wings, and pink skin rather than the almost bluish-violet skin that you will see on a recessive white canary. *(photo by Hans Classen)*

Chapter 20
Pertinent Points About Breeding Canaries

Sharing Experiences

If we are to advance our understanding of these delicate little songsters, it is up to us all to share and add to the common pool of knowledge. This is why I'd like to share with you some of the more valuable advice and insights on canaries that I've discovered or been taught over the years. Most of better tips are deceptively simple— the kind of thing that makes you wonder, *"Why didn't I think of that?"*

It is my hope that these pointers will be as great an

assistance to you as they were to me, and that you will make a point one day of passing them on in turn.

Canaries can be rather complicated little birds. Many's the successful finch, cockatiel, or budgie breeder I've seen advance with high hopes and cheerful dreams into the realm of breeding canaries, thinking that since they'd already mastered breeding one or more types of bird, how much more difficult could it be to raise the common canary? These people are almost always shocked to find that successfully raising healthy canaries is nowhere near as simple as they had blithely presumed it to be.

Countless new canary breeders have found themselves plagued with problems both major and minor. Problems are encountered getting the birds into condition to breed; once this is accomplished the balancing act continues, for now the birds must successfully incubate, hatch, and rear their young.

If their needs are not met, the attempt will fail.

Reasons for failure can include incorrect lighting or nutrition, egg-binding, infertile eggs, dead-in-shell, non-feeding parents, or even birds who will breed or feed themselves to death. The possible variations can seem endless; just when you think you've got it figured out, they will throw you another curve.

Daylight And Canaries

One of the most important things to understand about canaries is that they are photosensitive. They are affected by the changing lengths of the days in the temperate zones of the planet as the seasons progress through the year. Their bodies have evolved to allow them to adapt to the different environments created by the changing seasons, using exposure to light as the trigger.

This means that they become ready to breed in response to the physical stimulus that the lengthening days of springtime creates in their systems. Warmth and humidity have been shown to be secondary factors; they can aid in advancing the strength of the breeding response, but are not in themselves major factors.

Understanding that these birds are photosensitive means that the most reliable method of bringing them into breeding condition is to gradually increase the length of their days, beginning about three months before you wish to begin breeding. Keep the birds at about ten and a half hours of light a day for at least a month; this is their 'winter'.

Once their artificial 'winter' is over, begin increasing the length of their days in fifteen minute increments every week to week-and-a-half or so. If your timer is limited to half-hour increments, increase by a half hour every three weeks or thereabouts. Although you can rush the birds into breeding condition by increasing the day lengths faster, it is not a good idea for the long-term health of the birds, or the fertility of the eggs.

As the length of day hits eleven hours the birds will be active and busy, the hens in constant motion, the cocks singing heartily while pugnaciously trying to claim as much territory as possible. By the time twelve hours a day has arrived the hens are strewing nesting material everywhere; soon the eggs will begin to arrive, often around the same time the lights hit twelve hours a day.

Variable lighting and differing lengths of day can affect the canary's song, health, and moult, to the point of a long slow death if not corrected.
(photo by Michael de Freitas)

Some breeds of canary may need longer days to reach full breeding form, particularly the larger ones such as the Norwich, which reportedly can require daylengths of up to fourteen hours a day to successfully hatch and rear babies.

Continue increasing the light at a slow and steady pace until the birds have about fourteen hours of light per day. Hold it there during your breeding season, and then once the summer solstice has passed you can begin to gradually decrease the lengths of the days, again introducing a change in hours every two or three weeks, to encourage the annual moult to begin, which should begin within a month of the days beginning to grow shorter

Keep steadily reducing the length of the days until you have reached your winter marker of ten and a half hours, and then hold the days steady until midwinter, when it will again be time to begin the whole cycle anew, just in time for the next breeding season.

One final note; even if you only keep a single pet and never plan to breed him, you should try to give him some sense of the seasons, through increasing and decreasing days, to ensure that he moults properly every year. Scientists have shown that the canary species needs to experience this annual cycle in order to stay properly healthy, and that canaries who are deprived of experiencing these changes will generally die before reaching their second year.

Working With Canary Hens

Canary hens strengthen themselves for the stress and rigors of breeding season by flying. Her entire system depends on her body being as strong and healthy as possible before beginning the cycle of laying her eggs. If a canary hen is denied the opportunity to exercise through flying she could become physically unable to come into breeding condition, no matter how good her diet is or how long her days last.

The eggs she will lay will consist of up to 25% of her body mass. Her muscles will have to be strong and elastic in order to pass the eggs safely through her system. The muscles that perform this chore are the same muscles she uses to pull herself through the air. They are the main source of power for her wings, and run the entire length of her body from the keelbone to the sternum.

I try to allow my hens as much flight time as possible, in as large a space as possible, and they have always rewarded me with regular production of large, healthy clutches of eggs. I prefer a minimum flying space for a canary hen of three feet by two feet at least four feet tall— five to six feet tall is even better. It is my belief that the extra effort required to lift them to the top perches of a flight cage tall as well as broad strengthens them faster than horizontal flight.

In order to see that they don't get too flighty, they are periodically rotated into smaller breeding-sized cages of around fifteen inches high and tall, and about three feet long. Each hen usually spends about one week a month in the smaller cage, and the other three weeks in the flight cage until breeding season comes along. This also ensures that the necessary periodic health-inspection-and-toenail-clipping takes place on a regular basis.

The author's canary hens share two winter flights, connected by a 'pop-hole' through which they can move from one cage to the other, allowing them plenty of time flying. They take full advantage, and are constantly in motion. They're great fun to watch, too!

About Canary Eggs

Canary hens require calcium in order to form their eggs. This means that either cuttlebone, mineral gravel, or baked sterile eggshell bits must always be available to them. Some greens, such as spinach, beet greens, chard, and sorrel, contain fairly high levels of oxalic acid. This binds with and prevents the proper digestion of calcium, so such greens should not be fed when eggs are expected.

One important point to remember, is that the digestion of calcium requires Vitamin D to also be available within the bird's system, or the bird will not be able to digest the calcium. If the birds have access to sunshine that is *not* filtered through a glass window, or have full-spectrum lighting in their area, they will be fine, but if not then this essential vitamin *must* be provided for them.

Many other required elements are also not found in a regular bird diet, and so regular vitamin and mineral supplementation is a necessity for any keeper who desires a healthy flock. I prefer to use dry powdered vitamins. They are readily consumed when sprinkled lightly over soft foods, fruit, or greens.

Giving liquid vitamins in the water is an unreliable method to use with canaries, I find, as they break down quite swiftly once in the water, and the birds will probably not drink enough to be of much use to them in the short period of time the vitamins remain viable once in the water.

A useful tool that helps the birds produce their own Vitamin D in the same manner they do with sunshine is full-spectrum lighting. These lights are invaluable for indoor birds, and help to increase the general levels of health, well-being, and disease resistance.

They have been manufactured to emit light in the same spectrum as natural daylight. I feel that since our birds have evolved for thousands of years under this particular spectrum, who are we to try to improve on what Nature has adapted so well?

A final important fact to remember is that shortly before the chicks are due to hatch a rise in humidity is necessary. If it does not occur, the chick may be unable to penetrate the shell.

The easiest way to see that this happens when needed

is to be sure the hen has free access to her bath from the 11th day of incubation forward. Her instincts will guide her to provide the correct amount of moisture at precisely the correct time in order to assist her chicks in hatching out of their eggs, as long as you give her access to her bath.

Pairing Canaries

I find that it is usually easiest to breed canaries in pairs. The one thing that is always true about canary hens, though, is that each hen is a law unto herself. Her wants and needs, and her ways of expressing them, may be drastically different from her sister's. Some of my canaries have formed bonded pairs— I see this the most often in the Glosters and the Red canaries. If they are given the choice, such pairs will tend to stay near each other year round; where you see one, you can be sure the other is not far away.

A triple-dividable box breeding cage on top of a double-dividable box cage. For now the dividers are out, but can be slid into place whenever needed.

So far in my experience, pairs who are allowed to choose their own mates always make the best parents. Interestingly enough, science has recently and quite unexpectedly backed this idea up with the results of a study on mate fidelity done on wild canaries living on the Madeiran archipelago.

This study, published in 2006, showed that these birds were socially monogamous, unlike many other species of small songbird studied to date. DNA fingerprinting showed no evidence of extra-pair paternity, and their observations showed that the females actively rejected advances from males other than their mate.

Both parents actively cooperated to raise their young, and the team noted that biparental care appeared to be essential for offspring survival. Yet the DNA results showed no more sign of inbreeding than that of any other population of songbird studied, suggesting that the hens had studied and selected their chosen male outside of the breeding season, some time before it commenced.

So if at all possible, for me each breeding season begins with my choosing a group of reasonably compatible youngsters, and giving them a large flight cage to share for a few days, while I watch how they get along. If I see a pair forming, I make note of it, then move all the compatible pairs I've noted, each pair to their own breeding cage.

The assistance provided the hard-working canary hen by an affectionate and dedicated male cannot be over-emphasized. His help in feeding and especially weaning the chicks allows the hen to return to her nest and incubate a second clutch of chicks while the male weans the babies from the first.

This type of cooperation allows more babies to be produced with less stress on the hen, giving you overall improvement on the general level of health along with very good production of strong, healthy chicks.

Other pairs may hate each other at first sight, and yet may gradually accept each other (this is where cages with wire dividers come in handy), and yet other pairs will have nothing to do with each other no matter what you do.

The best advice I've ever received about solving problems with canary hens? An old-timer once told me *"I like to sit and watch 'em, and try to put myself in their place, try and understand what I'd want if I was them. Then I try to figger out what they'd tell me if they spoke English insteada Canary... then I* do it, and watch 'em to see how they like it. All ya gotta do is keep tryin' till ya get it right..."

It may sound simple, but simple observation can tell you volumes if you pay attention. The only guarantee you will have as you approach breeding season with these little beauties is that they will allow you to hone your sleuthing skills to the point where Sherlock Holmes' puzzles may just seem tame by comparison.

A Bad Night Can Ruin Your Day

If possible, try to arrange for a 'twilight' period of 5 to 15 minutes before turning your main lights off. An alternative is to give the birds a sound cue that darkness is coming.

A friend of mine has a radio in her birdroom on a separate timer from the lights; it is turned off about 15 minutes before her lights go out. The birds swiftly learned this sound cue, and now all of her hens are covering their eggs before her lights go out for the evening.

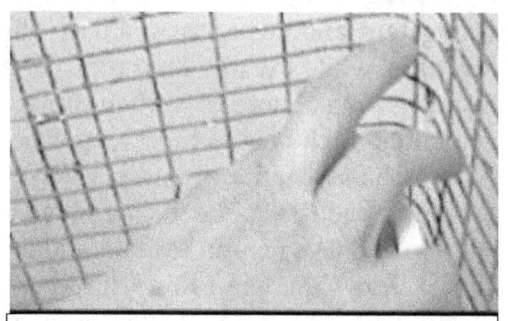

Replacing the nest after inspection and (if necessary) replacing eggs with dummies so the clutch may be set all at once, ensuring that the chicks will all hatch at close to the same time on the same day.

If the hen is not on the nest before the lights go out, the incubating embryos within the eggs may not survive, since canaries see little or nothing in the dark, and she may not be able to find her way back to her nest in the dark.

Some canary hens will do as their wild sisters do, and wait until the entire clutch is laid before they start brooding their eggs. But a wild canary has much more to do than a hen living in a cage, with all her needs provided. So sometimes a canary hen will begin incubating her eggs before the entire clutch is laid. This can result in a chick hatching every day over three or more days, and the result is all too often fatal for the younger, much-smaller chicks.

In order to prevent this, many breeders will take each egg away shortly after the hen has laid it, and replace it in the nest with a fake, or 'pot' egg. The eggs are handled gently from end-to-end, and stored safely until the hen's clutch is complete.

Any egg that crumbles upon being gently handled has too little calcium in the shell. If this should happen, check that the hen is using the supplies you have provided, whether cuttlebone, crushed baked eggshells, or mineral gravel, and check too that enough vitamins are present for proper digestion. Some hens may require extra vitamins and/or minerals supplements to be added to their food or water, in the form of drops or liquid concentrate.

Always make sure your hands are cleaned, rinsed, and dried before handling any eggs.

Moving or Handling The Eggs

Nests should always be hung so that they are easily removable. Canary hens usually lay their eggs early in the day, so wait until after the egg is laid and the hen has left the nest to eat her breakfast before you make your move. Then just quietly take the entire nest down and go with it into another room, away from where the hen can see you.

Gently remove the new egg, being careful to handle it correctly, and store it in a cup of dry stale seed, out of the sunlight and at room temperature, ideally no less than sixty-five degrees F and no more than eighty degrees. It will keep for several days, as long as the seed is dry and not oily. Do not use fresh seed, it's usually too oily, which can damage the eggshell's fragile balance, and don't use instant rice, it will dry the egg out.

Once the egg has been stored, you can go ahead and replace it in the nest with a pot egg, then parade the whole affair back to the cage, and hang the nest in its usual spot.

The hen will be so glad to see her nest back she will probably not notice that the egg has been switched, which is most definitely *not* the case (with some hens at least) if you do the switch where she can see you.

If you have more than one canary hen, make sure you label each clutch's container so as to make sure to return the right eggs to the right hen.

How do you know when the entire clutch is laid? Actually, that's one of the easiest parts. Most hens' final egg, once dry, will be bluer than the rest of the clutch. When you see the blue egg— once it's dried, the difference in colour is often quite distinct when you see it next to the previously-laid eggs— you'll know that her clutch is complete, and she will want to start incubating soon.

A normal-sized clutch of canary eggs varies from 3 to 5 eggs. 4 is common. This is a nest of canary eggs with the hen who laid them, showing how the nesting material builds up the nest and supports the eggs.

The average number of eggs to a clutch is four, but I have had hens who regularly laid three, five, or six eggs per clutch.

Setting The Eggs

Wait until you are certain that there will be no more eggs laid before allowing your hen to begin incubating her eggs. In the case of young hens, especially if she tends to be a little on the nervous side, I will often limit the clutch size to the first four eggs, and set her with one egg a day earlier than the other three. This way one chick will hatch a day early, giving the nervous young mother a chance to practice feeding one demanding young mouth instead of being suddenly overwhelmed by an entire nestful. The difference in size of one day between the elder and younger chicks will not be so drastic with the other three hatching together the following day.

Return the eggs to the hen in the early morning— the chicks should hatch roughly the same time of day that incubation begins, usually 13 or 14 days later, depending on how closely the hen sits on her eggs.

The more time she spends off the eggs, the later they will hatch. Incubation for any species is actually a set number of hours at a specific temperature. The embryo becomes dormant when the temperature drops whenever the hen leaves the nest; as long as she isn't gone for too long, the eggs will simply pause their development. When she returns and the temperature is again right, the embryo will resume developing. This adaptation allows a hen to leave her eggs long enough each day to eat and perform her other necessary duties without harming the growing chicks within the eggs.

Prolonged abandonment will kill the embryos inside the eggs, but it is not yet known for sure just how long they can survive away from the hen, once growth has begun.

This being the case, if I have to temporarily store eggs I hope to be live, I try to keep them at about 50 to 60 degrees F, and turn them a half turn lengthwise per day, rotating the egg gently using the large end as the bottom of a pivot. Do *not* turn the eggs side to side; this will do more harm than good.

Usually, if the hen is sett with her eggs first thing in the morning, the chicks will tend to hatch quite early in the day. Hatching in the morning allows them to receive the maximum possible amount of food before the end of their first day. This can make a world of difference regarding their ability to survive and thrive.

Finally, be sure to never have the days shorter than

twelve hours when there are (or you soon expect to have) chicks in the nest, as they may not survive a longer night.

Nesting Material

Burlap makes the best nesting material I have ever tried— and I'd be surprised to learn of any I'd not tried. To prepare burlap for use as nesting material first give it a thorough washing with soap and bleach in the washing machine; after this run the material through another cycle in plain water. Then cut it into 3-inch squares. You don't have to be exact, but smaller is better than large; try not to go over about three inches. Then shred each piece, pile the shredded material into a large bowl and pour boiling water over it. Stir it lightly to loosen the fibers, then leave it until it's cool enough for the fibers to be lifted out, lightly wrung, and spread to dry on a stack of newspapers.

A sign that the chicks are ready to band — droppings on the edge of the nest.

This may sound like a fair bit of work, but the end product is well worth it— a lovely, sterile, fluffy, light-beige material that the hens adore. They build fantastic nests with this material, and as it resists absorbing moisture, the hens can easily keep the nests clean until the chicks are old enough to lift their rear ends over the edge of the nest.

If the hen stops cleaning the nest and the chicks are not depositing on or over the edge, it means the nest is too deep. Take the nest and the chicks, place the chicks on a warm towel, and pack a bit of nesting material into the bottom of the nest. You want the depth of the nest to be about equal or a little less than the length of the youngsters' legs when extended. Return the chicks to the nest, and the nest to the parents, and everybody will be happier.

Banding The Babies

The chicks are the right age to band the first day they begin to deposit on the rim of the nest. Generally this is also when the hen stops cleaning the nest, so in this case there is no need to worry about her chucking foreign material out of the nest, as can happen when the chicks are banded too young. (All too often when this happens the 'foreign material' will still have the chick attached!)

If the hen is still cleaning the nest, then you must convince her that the band belongs where it is; I find the easiest way to do this is to band the chicks just before the lights go out for the day.

Make sure that the chicks have had their evening feeding, then take the entire nest into another room where you have some clean table

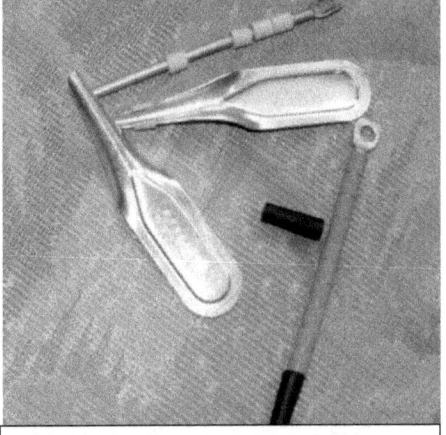

Open bands come in various colours, and can be applied at any age, unlike closed bands that must go on at 6 or so days old. These are shown with the tool used to apply them.

space, a good light, and a warm towel to set the chicks on. Keep your elbows on the table and the chick you are currently banding over the towel in case you accidentally drop it— it wouldn't be the first time a wriggly youngster has managed to squirm away!

The only kind of bands that needs applying at this age are the closed bands; open bands such as the ones shown above can be applied at any age. To apply a closed band, carefully fold the chicks three forward-facing toes together and slip the band over them onto the youngster's leg, pulling the back-ward pointing toe gently out of the band.

If the band does not fit over the ball of the foot, you are using too small a band; get some that are a size larger. A canary's leg will thicken a bit as the bird ages, and you don't want problems caused a year or too down the line if the band becomes too small! When you have all the chicks banded, return them to the nest and return the nest to the parents just before the lights are due to go out.

If you time it right, she will just have time to check that her chicks are all there and hop aboard before the lights go out for the evening. In the morning she should ignore the bands on her babies legs as if they had been there all along. I have had several occasions to use this trick, and, as long as I time it properly, it has worked every time.

Finally, when you buy your bands, also buy a band cutter, in case you may someday need it. Practice using it by placing extra bands onto a green willow stick. Then practice cutting the bands off until you can do it without leaving a mark on the green willow bark; this way you will know you can remove a closed band from a canary's leg without harm.

These tips are some of the best advice ever given me. I would not be breeding canaries today if it were not for the folks who took it upon themselves to help out the rank beginner that I was. Rather than keeping the 'secrets' of their success to themselves, they spent time and effort educating me. I didn't realize it then, but that in itself was one of the greatest gifts of all— no one who breeds canaries ever has much if any time to spare!

So go ahead and use these tips, but don't stop there. Share them with another bird keeper when you have the chance, and that way we will all continue to benefit from the growth of our shared knowledge. Ultimately, it's your birds who will thank you, in more ways than you can imagine.

Mom and Dad with two just-fledged 'squeakers'; these left the nest at 17 days old, but it would have been just as normal if they had fledged several days later, the timing can vary from 17 to 30 days or so.

Chapter 21
Weaning Youngsters

Weaning young canaries can be nerve-wracking for the humans involved, especially if you're new to keeping canaries. This is a delicate time for the youngsters. They must succeed at the transition from being fed by their parents to eating on their own, or they will not survive to grow to adulthood. And all too often, at the same time the chicks start to experiment with eating for themselves, the adult canaries will decide that they *must* have another nest.

If the chicks being weaned are from the first nest of the season, that's fine. If the father is with his family and is feeding his babies, you can go ahead and put a new nest at the far end of the cage and provide some nesting material for the hen to use. Watch her carefully to be sure that she doesn't decide that she likes the chick's feathers better than the nesting material you have provided, and decide to use them instead! If she does, put a wire divider between her and the rest of the family. You can remove it for an hour or so every morning so the adults may mate.

In this scenario, the male will finish weaning the babies, while his hen begins another nest. But sometimes you will have a hen raising her babies alone. In this case, remove the nest as soon as the chicks leave it, and don't offer it again until the chicks are actually weaned and eating on their own unless you have to— you will know when that is, because the hen will make it obvious that she is going to refurbish a seedcup or even a spot on the floor, if necessary.

If that is the case, I go ahead and let her have her nesting material and a new nest, but I'll watch carefully to see that she keeps tending to her babies. Most hens will continue to feed the youngsters if they need it, even while working on a new nest.

Some, though, may not. In that case I'll remove the new nest entirely, along with any feed cups that could possibly be sat in. I offer a large variety of soft foods on a paper plate on the floor of the cage with only two perches in the cage, set just a few inches above floor level.

That way the chicks will be walking on soft food whenever they set food on the floor, and this will stimulate their instinct to peck. As soon as they figure out that what they are standing on is actually food, you will know you're past the worst of it— the chicks should be fine, once they have made that so-important mental connection.

If the hen continues to pluck, put a wire divider between her and the chicks, to restrain her passion for nest-building materials to those you have provided.

As long as both she and the chicks have a wide variety of foods to tempt them, and she has nothing better to do, she should continue to feed the chicks through the wire divider, topping up their hunger while they experiment with eating, but she will not be able to pluck them, except perhaps for the odd facial feather.

If the chicks being weaned are from the second nest of the season, there's another issue to deal with as well as weaning the youngsters. Your bird-parents will not want to take a rest from breeding until the breeding hormones stop circulating, and their body enters the start of the annual moult. Normally this will happen shortly after mid-summer, two or three weeks after the solstice has passed and the days begin to get shorter. If the season is not quite that advanced yet but you think your pair has had more than enough babies, you might want to consider another tactic often resorted to by canary breeders in order to keep their birds from exhausting themselves raising too many chicks.

Once the second nest of youngsters has been reared, go ahead and allow the hen to build a third nest and even lay a third clutch of eggs, if she insists, and go ahead and swap her eggs for the fake plastic canary eggs mentioned a few pages above. These fake eggs are generally not too difficult to procure, and are readily available from suppliers such as Redbird or Silversong West.

Then, instead of giving her real eggs back to her once the clutch is complete,

Some useful containers for seed, treats, soft foods and other such items. Note the plain paper plates, very useful anytime, but even more so when it is hot and/or you're offering foods that can go sour or develop moulds.

leave her to sett on the fake eggs until a week or two after midsummer before you remove her nest. By then the annual moult will be due to start soon, and she should be more willing to abandon the idea of further nests in the current year. Meanwhile you will not have to worry about any more hatchlings.

The need to deal with this sort of occasion is one reason I believe it is important to not start breeding too early in the year, as if the birds can see any natural daylight at all, they will not want to stop breeding before midsummer. The reason that can be a problem is because too long and stressful a breeding season can mean a very rough moult for the birds, and often a poor breeding season next year as well. In fact, if they lose enough energy, they may never recuperate properly; such a hen may never breed properly again.

Once the youngsters begin to eat on their own and stop crying to be fed, you can move them into a 'nurse' cage. This is a plain, safe cage with lots of floor space and low perches. Once you are sure the chicks are eating well on their own, they can go from here into a small flight cage, to learn the skills of flying.

Flying is to canaries, what walking is to human children. It's a skill that must be learned in childhood, to be learned properly; if for whatever reason the youngsters don't learn to fly when they are young, they will never learn the finer points of flying. It's very important to their psyche to learn to fly at this age, so even if it's only temporary, try to give them this experience if at all possible.

Generally the parents will keep feeding their young for awhile even after they start to experiment with eating on their own, so as long as the chicks are still being fed, even if it's only part of the time, I tend to leave the family together. There should be no problems as long as they aren't still there when new chicks hatch out; in that case the hen will attempt to drive the older chicks away.

Be careful not to offer too much high-protein food to the weanling chicks, such as you gave the parents when the chicks were still in the nest and growing rapidly. Instead offer only a little, and supplement that with plenty of dark leafy greens daily, things like kale, leafy endives, mustard greens, dandelions, and other such foods— they offer good quantities of vitamins and minerals, and are also high in trace nutrients and elements that are so very important for the swiftly-growing young canary bodies.

Other useful weanling foods are rolled oats, plain prepared couscous, and soak seed. Remember, often a canary youngster will not be physically able to crack enough dry seed to fully support himself until he is around twelve weeks (three months) old, so be sure to keep a variety of soft foods around until they have finished their baby moult,

The first moult is the only time in their life that a canary will not moult out all his or her feathers. The 'baby' moult, as it is usually known, starts when the chicks are six to eight weeks old, and will last for another six to eight weeks, during which time the youngsters will replace all of their small body feathers; but not the wing and tail feathers. Thus these youngsters are known as 'unflighted' canaries. They will not replace their wing or tail feathers until their first complete moult, at just over a year old; at that point they will become known as 'flighted' canaries.

I prefer to use a slightly modified soaked-seed-and-nestling-food mix when weaning youngsters, as I find it makes the process quite easy if done correctly. It is less dangerous, too, as a higher-protein nestling food can go bad before it smells or tastes off, especially in hot weather. Sour foods can cause e-coli infections, or worse.

A group of the author's young canaries; most have just finished bathing, and are busily preening.

It's a very simple modification— as stated in Chapter 18, I begin to cut back on the amount of dry pabulum added to the nestling food mix once the chicks are out of the nest, until by a few weeks later there is none at all in the mixture. This reduces both the overall protein content and also the speed at which the mix will go sour.

If you are using a commercial nestling food, you can make a reasonable weaning food by mixing it in equal parts with dry ground whole-wheat breadcrumbs before adding it to the soak seed. See Chapter 18 for more detail on this.

When weaning, you also want to offer foods with a higher starch content and less protein than what you used while they were in the nest, but still with strong vitamin and mineral content.

I use lots of dark leafy greens, like kale, leafy mustard, leafy endives, etcetera– not much spinach, sorrel, or chard, as they interfere with proper digestion of calcium, and the chicks need that for their still-growing bones. I also see that the youngsters always have dry rolled oats on hand. These are easy to eat, and will give them lots of easily digested calories. If you can afford them, you can also use crunched up cereals such as corn flakes, shredded wheat or cheerios (use the unsweetened cereals, of course!).

Prepared couscous is useful too. Use the plain unflavoured kind. You can even make it using juice instead of water. Most birds will peck at it, and it can to help get some weight onto the youngsters. Just be aware that too much couscous over too long a time will see you wind up with a chubby little 'perch potato'.

Offer this variety of foods on a wide flat paper plate, and lower all the perches so that they are close to the floor and the plate– that way it will be very obvious exactly where the food is to be found. The more the youngsters have to walk on the food you have offered them, the sooner they will be tempted to eat it. Soft footing stimulates the pecking instinct– the chick pecks, and learns that it is standing on food. A plain paper plate is ideal for offering these kinds of soft foods, since they will not sour as fast as they do in a cup or dish, instead just tending to dry out.

Robirda McDonald

This canary's interesting plumage is created by the combination of two recessive mutations, and is known as 'phaeo-ino'. *(photo by Hans Classen)*

Chapter 22
Basic Canary Colours & Genetics

It is not my intention to give you anything more than a brief introduction to canary genetics here— if you find this chapter wets your thirst for a deeper understanding of canary genetics, I recommend you read the books listed in the bibliography at the end of this book, in particular Geoff Walker's excellent book, 'Coloured, Type, and Song Canaries'.

Basic Canary Colours

Before we go into canary genetics, let me give you a brief rundown on the basics of the kinds of colours you will find in canaries. There is two parts to a canary's colour; the lipochrome or 'ground' colour, and the melanin colours, which may or may not be present even if the canary has the genetic ability to show them.

Lipochrome (Ground) Colours

Briefly, lipochrome colours are derived from the food a canary eats. They are in essence, fatty acids removed from the foods and placed in the feathers by the canary's bloodstream, while the feathers are growing in.

There is four ground colours in canaries; yellow, red, and white, which occurs in two forms; dominant white, and recessive white. Then another mutation occurred that caused an optical illusion of making the ground colour paler; this became known as 'ivory', which creates three more lipochrome colours, ivory yellow, sometimes called 'gold ivory, and ivory red, also known as 'rose'. The third is ivory white, but is rarely seen and even more rarely recognized.

So, all canaries have a ground colour, and only one ground colour; you can't have a canary that is, say, both red ground and yellow ground (although it is possible for a canary to look that way, but that's due to incorrect colour-feeding). So you have;

- Yellow ground canaries
- Red ground canaries
- White ground canaries (whether dominant or recessive)
- Ivory ground canaries (whether yellow ivory, red ivory, or white ivory)

Melanin Colours

Besides lipochrome and feather structure, melanin plays a central part in the visual appearance of any canary. Melanin, or lack of it, can affect almost all visual aspects of a canary's appearance.

Canaries that show melanin in their feathers are often termed 'classic' coloured canaries. There are three colours of melanin seen in the wild canary; black, dark brown, and light brown, and any of them, separately or together, or for that matter, none of them, may show up in a domestic canary's feathers at any one time, offering a great deal of visual variety in melanistic canaries.

Canaries that show all three melanin colours on a yellow ground colour exhibit the same colour as the original wild canaries; this colour of canary is usually called 'black yellow', or, 'green'. The same group of melanins on a red ground canary is known as 'red-black', or, bronze, while the same three melanins appearing on a white-ground canary will be termed 'white-black', or, 'blue'.

When these melanins occur on an ivory-ground bird, the term 'ivory' is simply appended to the non-mutated colour; i.e., rose ivory plus a full complement of melanin is known as a 'red-black ivory'.

There are two common melanin mutations that offer yet more combinations of colour. First, the brown or 'cinnamon' mutation occurred, in which the black melanins are suppressed, and all that shows on the feathers are the dark and light browns. These birds also possess a dark plum-coloured eye, rather than the black eye seen normally, and because the black has been repressed they have paler skin, beak, and toes than the black-yellow or black-red canaries..

The second melanin mutation is the 'agate', or 'dilute' mutation, which reduced the width of the black melanin striations on the feather, and diluted the black pigmentation on the skin, beak, and such, leaving little pigment behind. The effect is an almost silvery-gray canary with fine black striations.

When combined with the brown mutation, the agate produces the 'isabel' or 'dilute brown', in which most of the visual melanins are suppressed, leaving only faint brown striations showing on the lipochrome ground colour.

Most of these classic melanin mutations will only occur alone. You can't have, for example, a black-red canary that is also an agate. So you have;
- ground colour + all melanins = (colour)-black, i.e., yellow-black, red-black, ivory-black, white-black (also known, in order, as green, bronze, ivory-bronze, and blue)
- Ground colour plus mutated brown melanins = (colour)-brown, i.e., yellow-brown, red-brown, ivory-brown, white-brown (also known as

cinnamon, red brown, ivory brown, and fawn).
> Ground colour + dilute mutated melanins (agate) = (colour)-agate, i.e., yellow agate, red agate, gold or rose ivory agate, white agate.

There are other known mutations that can occur, usually the name of such a mutation is simply appended to the 'classic' description. At this time the other recognized mutations that currently occur in canaries are known as Pastel, Ino, Sattinette, Opal, Onyx, Topaz, Cobalt, and Eumo.

Originally, all canaries were melanistic. But as more generations of canaries were kept in captivity, first canaries with light-coloured patches (these days usually known as 'variegation') occurred, & eventually canaries that showed no melanin at all arrived— and the colour that most of the world these days thinks all canaries look like was born, the yellow canary. This 'new colour' canary so enthralled the world's population that the colour became a synonym for the name of the bird, and the term 'canary yellow' has been around ever since.

The popular conception is that all canaries are yellow, but they actually come in a wide variety of kinds and colours. *(photo by Hans Classen)*

The complete lack of visible melanin in the feathers produces what is usually termed a 'clear' canary, that is, one that shows only it's lipochrome colour, whether white, ivory, red, or yellow. But what is not always understood is that the ability to show the melanins is still there, and the melanins themselves are still present in the bird's body; they are simply visually suppressed in the feathers, not eliminated.

Together, these lipochrome ground colours and the classic melanin colours form the groundwork for most of the canary colours you will commonly see today.

Types of Mutations Found in Canaries

Besides the different types of feathering, which can affect a canary's appearance, canary mutations can be found which you will hear being referred to as *Gender-Linked Recessive*, *Heterozygous Dominant*, and *Homozygous Recessive*.

Don't be afraid of these horrendous-sounding words—the principles behind them are actually fairly straightforward, and need to be mastered, if you are going to gain a basic understanding of canary genetics.

Male canaries carry a pair of chromosomes known as *XX*, while the hen's chromosomes are known as *XY*. (Yes, this is opposite to the pattern found in mammals). Some scientists instead use the letters *Z* and *W* to designate the different genes in birds, reasoning that since birds are so very different from mammals, a different system should be used, to promote greater accuracy.

This would mean that a male canary would be *WW*, while a hen would be *WZ*. In order to prevent confusion, I have stayed in this chapter with the better-known '*X*' and '*Y*' designations.

When a mutated gene must be present on each side of the chromosome halves in order to express itself visibly, the mutation is known as *Homozygous Recessive*, meaning that the genes on each side of the chromosome are the same.

In most cases, when a mutated gene needs only to be present in one of the bird's two chromosomes to affect the bird's appearance, it is known as a *Heterozygous Dominant* mutation, meaning that the gene must be present only in one location for the mutation to be visible in the bird's feathers.

The exceptions to this generality are the *Gender-Linked Recessive* mutations, where the mutated gene need only be carried on the hen's X chromosome to be visible, as if it were a dominant. (This is why this type of mutation was, for a time, known as a *sub-dominant* mutation.)

However, the same mutation, when present on only one of the male's X chromosomes, does not change his appearance at all, acting as if it was a recessive gene. For a male canary to visually show a Gender-Linked Recessive mutation, he must carry the mutation on both of his X chromosomes. This in turn means that he must receive the mutated gene from both his parents in order to visually display the mutated colour. In other words, in the male canary the mutated gene acts as a recessive, instead of appearing to be dominant, as in the hens.

a 'mosaic', showing the distinctive facial 'mask' so reminiscent of a goldfinch, lacking in hens with this feather type.   *(photo by Hans Classen)*

What causes this seeming contradiction is the fact that the gene that causes this mutation is located in the same area of the chromosome that defines gender, leading to this rather confusing group of mutations being termed *Gender-Linked Recessives*.

Feather Type

Feather type can dramatically affect a canary's appearance, a fact a lot of people don't at first realize. The same colour mutation can appear to be a rather different-looking bird, depending on which type of feathering it has. There are three basic types of feather type, in canaries – four, if you count the mutation which curls the feathers and produces the different varieties of frilled canaries. As this mutation is only seen in frilled breeds, though, it is not considered a separate feather type.

As with many things in life, some canaries have feathers that don't fall exactly into any one of these categories. Others may have one type of feather in one area of their bodies, and a different type of feather in others. A few others may have feathers that show characteristics of two of these types combined.

These birds are the exception rather than the rule, however, and in general most canaries' feathering can be classed as being distinctly of one type or another.

These three feather types are known as *Intensive* (often called *hard-feathered*, or, *yellow*), Non-intensive (also called *soft-feathered*, or, *buff*), and *Dimorphic* (also called *mosaic*)

Intensive Feathers

This feather type is often called a *hard-feathered* bird, or even, by some old-timers, *yellow*. This last term actually refers not to the colour yellow, but to the feather structure. The two most common feather types in canaries were originally known as *yellow* and *buff*.

The most prized canary colour in earlier days was the clear yellow bird, mutated from the more common green. The hard-feathered bird appeared to be a much more intensive colour of yellow in these birds, so 'yellow' was a natural enough name for this feather type, at first.

When canary colours grew to include various other

shades such as red, rose, and white, along with increasingly various melanin shades, many people changed the feather terms they were using to *hard-feathered* and *soft-feathered*, because of the ease of confusion of the feather-structure term *yellow* with the colour yellow.

These days the terms considered most correct when discussing feather type are *intensive* for the 'hard' or 'yellow' type of feather, and *non-intensive* for the feather type previously called 'buff', or 'soft-feathered'. But you will still hear the older terms all used fairly frequently, too, and probably will for some years yet.

In the intensively feathered canaries, the feather colour extends right to the edge of the feathers, giving the bird's colour a deep, rich solid effect to the eye— a 'harder' colour, if you will.

These two variegated canaries share the same ground colour, but have different feather types; the one on the right is intensive, while the one on the left is non-intensive. *(photo by Michael de Freitas)*

Each feather narrows a little towards the tip, and the feathers overall are slightly narrower than those found on canaries of the other feather types.

This tends to make the birds appear to be a little slimmer in outline than birds of other feather type, and can make them appear to be overall a little smaller than they actually are, too.

Usually breeders try to breed a canary with non-intensive feathers to one with intensive feathering. This ensures that a roughly even distribution of feather types will be maintained in the offspring.

This can be quite important, as it has been shown that breeding intensively feathered birds together will, with each generation gradually reduce the feather width until the feathers are so scant that the skin begins to show through in places.

Non-Intensive Feathers

In a non-intensively-feathered canary, the feather itself is slightly broader, and more rounded at the tip, while the colour does not cover the entire area of the web— there is a small band or edging on each feather which in a canary lacking melanins will appear white, while in the darker canaries, such as the canary shown at the top of page 156, will be greyish.

This 'fringe', when lapped over the feathers underneath, softens the intensity of the colour (thus the common name of 'soft' feather), and gives the bird a generally softer look to the colour, and a slightly rounder appearance.

A canary with non-intensive feathers should preferably be bred to a mate with intensive feathering, so that a full complement of both feather types will be maintained in the offspring.

Breeding non-intensive feathered birds together over several generations will see each generation showing slightly broader feathers, and is thought to contribute to a tendency for developing feather lumps.

These are feathers that don't manage to break through the skin while forming, and instead cause a huge swelling under the skin. This is disfiguring, and can be dangerous if it puts too much pressure on a vital area.

Dimorphic Feathers

The third feather mutation is known as the *dimorphic*, or sometimes *mosaic* feather. It is a fully recessive mutation, in which the feather is broader even than the non-intensive feather, and the lipochrome colour is restricted to a small area in the very center of the feather.

This leaves a broad edging on each feather, with the visual result of the colourless edges overlapping each other so that very little lipochrome colour is visible to the eye. A dimorphic lipochrome canary will appear to be almost white, with bright colour points, while a dimorphic melanin canary will appear quite grey, but again, have brightly coloured points. In fact, a good dimorphic canary will have noticeable lipochrome colour only on the rump just above the tail, the butts of the wings, and in the males, a distinctive blaze around the eyes (usually known as a *mask*.)

Canaries can show several recessive colour mutations at once, such as the hen shown here who has four mutations, two gender-linked recessive, two recessive; she is a rose agate mosaic pastel canary hen.   *(photo by Hans Classen)*

One interesting fact about this mutation is that it is the *only* breed of canary in which it is usually possible to reliably discern the gender of a given canary based on its visual appearance. Due to a quirk of the dimorphic feather structure, a male dimorphic canary will display a distinctive blaze of colour around the eyes, almost like the mask seen on a goldfinch, while the hen shows little to no facial colour.

In the melanistic colours, the broadness of the feather

leads to the normally fainter striations on the breast and flanks being less distinct than those on an intensive or non-intensive melanin canary.

Inheritance Patterns

In these examples, 'normal' is considered to be a bird showing any of the basic colours or kinds, without any other mutations being present, either hidden or visual. For the purpose of the examples, we will assume that paired birds will have complementary feather types.

Normal x Normal: 'Normal' canaries can be any canary not showing a specific mutation. Such a canary could be Red, Yellow, Black-Red, Black-Yellow, or a Red or Yellow-ground variegate. The expectations with such a pairing are 100% normal offspring, assuming that neither partner carries any Recessive or (in the male's case) Gender-Linked Recessive mutations.

Normal x Dominant: Probably the most commonly seen Dominant mutations are the Crest, and the Dominant White lipochrome colour. When the Dominant White occurs in a dark (or *melanistic*) canary, it is known as a *Black-White* or *Blue* canary. Normal x Dominant is the most desirable mating when looking to pair a bird showing a Dominant mutation. You can expect to get 50% normal offspring, and 50% dominant offspring, of both genders.

Dominant x Dominant: This is not a recommended pairing, because 25% of the offspring produced may be born deformed or die still in the egg, or worse, shortly after hatching. Expectations are 25% normal offspring, 50% dominant offspring, and 25% dead-in-shell (or nest). Note that this pairing produces the same number of white youngsters— 50% Dominant offspring— as the Dominant x Normal pairing.

Gender-Linked Recessive mutations:

There are a number of Gender-Linked Recessive mutations, and I won't attempt to mention them all here—

for more detail, see Geoff Walker's excellent canary reference, recommended at the end of this book.

Some of the Gender-Linked Recessive mutations have been around for quite some time now. The *Agate,* the *Isabel,* and the *Cinnamon* are good examples— French writer Hervieux de Chanteloupe in his book "Traite aux Serins" (The Traits of Serins), mentions cinnamon canaries as far back as 1709.

Cinnamon is an older name for this mutation, and in order to cause less confusion, these days is often known more simply as *Brown*. A cinnamon canary can be a *Red-Brown* when it appears in a red ground canary, a *yellow-Brown* in the yellow ground birds, and *White-Brown* (or *Fawn*) when seen in white canaries, whether dominant or recessive white.

This canary shows the dominant mutation that causes the crest, also called the topknot, to appear.
(photo by Michael de Freitas)

A mutation described as similar to the canary today known as the *Agate Canary* was described along with the Cinnamon canaries in early French bird-keeping literature, but it appears that this particular colour mutation eventually died out. The modern Agate canaries we know today come from a mutation that was documented to have occurred in Holland in 1900.

The *Ivory* mutation is another popular Gender-Linked Recessive mutation, first documented in Holland in the early 1950's. The Ivory mutation is known as *Red Ivory, Rose* or *Rose Ivory* when it occurs in Red-ground canaries, *Ivory* or *Yellow Ivory* when it occurs in yellow canaries, while in white canaries, although rare, it is known as *White Ivory*.

Normal male x Gender-Linked Recessive hen: This pairing will product 50% Normal male young, all carrying the Gender-Linked Recessive mutation, and 50% normal hens.

Normal hen x Gender-Linked Recessive Male: This is an interesting pairing, because it is possible to tell the gender of the youngsters while still in the nest. Expectations are for 50% Normal male young, all carrying the Gender-Linked Recessive mutation, and 50% Gender-Linked Recessive hens.

Normal male carrying Gender-Linked Recessive x Normal hen: This pairing will allow you to know the gender of 25% of the offspring while still in the nest. Expectations are for 25% Gender-Linked Recessive female chicks, 25% Normal female chicks, 25% Normal male chicks, and 25% Normal males carrying the Gender-Linked Recessive mutation. Test mating will be required to separate the Normal males carrying the Gender-Linked Recessive gene from the Normal males who do not; there will be no visual difference.

Normal male carrying Gender-Linked Recessive x Gender-Linked Recessive hen: With this pairing you can expect to see 25% Normal males carrying the Gender-Linked Recessive gene, 25% visual Gender-Linked Recessive males, 25% Normal hens, and 25% Gender-Linked Recessive hens. This pairing is considered useful for keeping the strain strong.

Gender-Linked Recessive x Gender-Linked Recessive: This pairing is predictable, but if pursued for too many generations may result in a weak line. Expected results are 100% Gender-Linked Recessive offspring, of both genders.

Recessive mutations

There are some wonderful recessive mutations in the Canary family. Many of these are found in the group known as *New Colour Canaries*. Among these you will find such mutations as the *Ino*, the *Opal*, and the *Topaz*. *Recessive White* is another popular recessive mutation, and the *Dimorphic* or *Mosaic* mutation, that alters the shape of the feather, is also a recessive mutation.

Normal x Recessive: This is a fairly simple pairing to predict—the offspring will be 100% Normal birds of both genders. All offspring will carry the mutated Recessive gene, but none will show it visually.

Normal Carrying Recessive x Normal: This is not a recommended pairing, because test mating of the young in the following year will have to occur before the chick's genetic inheritance will be known for sure. All of the offspring of a pairing of this kind will appear Normal, but 25% of them will carry the Recessive gene.

This hen shows a bit of variegation around the eyes; this is usually known as a 'tick'. *(photo by Mike de Freitas)*

Most matings like this probably occur accidentally, due to the breeder not knowing that one of his birds carries a Recessive gene. Such a gene can be carried for dozens of generations in this manner, without ever becoming visibly present, unless a carrier should accidentally happen to be mated with another bird who also carries the same Recessive gene, allowing the recessive gene to express itself. Such happenings underscore the importance of keeping good breeding records!

Normal Carrying Recessive x Recessive: This is a recommended pairing for those who wish to keep a strong healthy line of Recessive birds in their bird-rooms. Recessive x recessive matings carried out each generation can drastically weaken the strength, colour intensity, and overall vigour of the breeding stock if pursued for more than a few generations.

A mild out-crossing such as this one helps maintain the size, vigour, and good feather colour of the entire group, while retaining the desired recessive mutation in the flock. Expectations from this pairing are 50% visibly Recessive offspring, of both genders, and 50% Normal offspring, of both genders. All of the visually normal offspring will carry the Recessive gene, even though they don't show it.

Recessive x Recessive: This pairing is the one considered the most desirable by many new breeders, as it offers highly predicable results— the offspring, of either gender, will be 100% the same mutation as their parents.

However, as mentioned above, crossing Recessive to Recessive for too many generations has been documented to often lead to smaller, weaker, less colourful birds. In the interest of maintaining a strong, healthy flock, I recommend alternating this kind of pairing with the pairing above every other year, alternating between the two kinds of pairing.

This should help maintain the overall health and vigour of the entire flock, while still producing a fair number of visually Recessive birds to enhance your aviaries and win you ribbons and trophies at shows.

Recommended Reading

In my opinion, these are the best resources you'll find anywhere on keeping and breeding canaries. In all likelihood, you will not be able to just walk into a bookstore and buy one. Some can be difficult to find, but once you have them you will be glad you took the time to acquire these so-useful resources!

Colour, Type & Song Canaries, by G.B.R. Walker & Dennis Avon. This is the 'Bible' of canary aficionados everywhere. It is loaded with detailed information on all aspects of care, breeding, and showing of canaries, and features an insert full of full-colour photos by world-class photographer Dennis Avon. A must-have for any serious canary keeper, one you will refer to time and again over the years.

Canary Breeding Tips and Tricks, by Herman Osman
Although first published in 1955, so that much of the nutritional information is out-of date, this book contains a wealth of advice and ideas on canary management and handling. You'll find practical specifics on dealing with many of the challenges facing a canary keeper. Filled to the brim with insight born of a lifetime of breeding canaries, this is a book no canary lover should miss.

The Complete Book of Canaries, by G.T. Dodwell.
An encyclopedic book loaded with beautiful, detailed pictures and multitudes of excellent full-colour photos, this book defines many aspects and terms to do with canaries, from early husbandry & history to shows & breeding. Beautiful & informative.

Canary Tales, by Linda Hogan
A self-published book loaded with detailed canary care information, by a well known and respected Roller Canary judge and breeder. Available online at canarytales.blogspot.com.

A Place For Canaries, at www.robirda.com
An ever-growing resource for anything canary, this is the place to look for answers to Frequently Asked Questions, great articles, photos, and Canary Cam pics to browse through, find Robirda's famous Canary Song CD, "New Songs From The Birdroom", learn about upcoming books and products, and more!

CPSIA information can be obtained
at www.ICGtesting.com
Printed in the USA
BVHW030108090722
641728BV00013B/1168